Science

Detailed Explanation to all Objective
& Subjective Problems

Science

Detailed Explanation to all Objective & Subjective Problems

7

Kriti Sharma • Seema Mehra • Sikha Sharma

卐 Administrative & Production Offices

Corporate Office: 'Ramchhaya' 4577/15, Agarwal Road, Darya Ganj, New Delhi -110002
Tele: 011- 47630600, 43518550; Fax: 011- 23280316

Head Office: Kalindi, TP Nagar, Meerut (UP) - 250002
Tele: 0121-2401479, 2512970, 4004199; Fax: 0121-2401648

All disputes subject to Meerut (UP) jurisdiction only.

卐 Sales & Support Offices

Agra, Ahmedabad, Bengaluru, Bhubaneswar, Bareilly, Chennai, Delhi, Guwahati, Haldwani Hyderabad, Jaipur, Jalandhar, Jhansi, Kolkata, Kota, Lucknow, Meerut, Nagpur & Pune

卐 ISBN 978-93-5251-150-1

卐 Price : ₹ 75

PRINTED & BOUND BY
ARIHANT PUBLICATIONS (I) LTD. (PRESS UNIT)

For further information about the products from Arihant
log on to www.arihantbooks.com or email to info@arihantbooks.com

PREFACE

The Department of Education in Science & Mathematics (DESM) & National Council of Educational Research & Training (NCERT) developed Exemplar Problems in Science and Mathematics for Upper Primary Stage, Secondary and Senior Secondary Classes with the objective to provide the students a large number of quality problems in various forms and format viz. Multiple Choice Questions, Short Answer Questions, Long Answer Questions etc., with varying levels of difficulty.

The problems given in Exemplar books are not meant to some merely as question bank for examination but are Primarily meant to improve the quality of teaching/ learning process in schools and finally will impart the problem solving skills in students and it is a widely at acknowledged fact that in this century analytical thinking, problem solving ability, creativity and speculative ability will be key skills for success.

This book **NCERT Exemplar Problems-Solutions Science VII** contains Explanatory & Accurate Solutions to all the questions given in NCERT Exemplar Science book.

For the overall benefit of the students we have made unique this book in such a way that it presents not only hints and solutions but also detailed and authentic explanations. Through these detailed explanations, students can learn the concepts which will enhance their thinking and learning abilities.

For the completion of this book, we would like to thank Mr. Prince Mittal (Project Coordinator, Arihant Prakashan) who helped us at project management level.

With the hope that this book will be of great help to the students, we wish great success to our readers.

Authors

CONTENTS

1

Nutrition in Plants

Multiple Choice Questions (MCQs)

Q. 1 Organisms which prepare food for themselves using simple naturally available raw materials are referred to as

(a) heterotrophs
(b) autotrophs
(c) parasites
(d) saprophytes

Ans. *(b)* **Autotrophs** are organisms that make food themselves from simple substances like water, CO_2 in the presence of sunlight and chlorophyll, e.g. Green plants.

Heterotrophs are organism, which cannot make their own food and take in food prepared by the plants, e.g. Animals and humans.

Parasites are organisms, which live and derive nutrition from another organism, called host, e.g. *Cuscuta* plant.

Saprophytes are organism, which obtain nutrition from dead & decaying organic matter, e.g. Fungi, bacteria, etc.

Q. 2 In the absence of which of the following will photosynthesis not occur in leaves?

(a) Guard cells
(b) Chlorophyll
(c) Vacuole
(d) Space between cells

Ans. *(b)* Chlorophyll is the green pigment present in leaves of plants that absorbs sunlight energy, to carry out photosynthesis. In the absence of chlorophyll, the leaves would not be able to capture sunlight energy. Therefore, no photosynthesis can occur.

Q. 3 Which of the following statements is/are correct?

(i) All green plants can prepare their own food.
(ii) Most animals are autotrophs.
(iii) Carbon dioxide is not required for photosynthesis.
(iv) Oxygen is liberated during photosynthesis.

Choose the correct answer from the options below:

(a) (i) and (iv)
(b) only (ii)
(c) (ii) and (iii)
(d) (i) and (ii)

Ans. ***(a)*** Statements (i) and (iv) are correct. All green plants are autotrophs. They can make their own food from simple substances like CO_2 and H_2O by the process of photosynthesis. Oxygen gas produced during this process is liberated into the air.

The other statements in correct form are:

Most animals are heterotrophs and CO_2 is essential for photosynthesis.

Q. 4 Pitcher plant traps insects because it

(a) is a heterotroph
(b) grows in soils which lack in nitrogen
(c) does not have chlorophyll
(d) has a digestive system like human beings

Ans. ***(b)*** Pitcher plant is an insectivorous plant that grow only in soils which do not contain sufficient nitrogen. These plants trap insects by various methods, kill them and digest then to obtain nitrogen compounds for their growth.

Q. 5 The terms that is used for the mode of nutrition in yeast, mushroom and bread mould is

(a) autotrophic (b) insectivorous (c) saprophytic (d) parasitic

Ans. ***(c)*** Saprophytic nutrition is seen in yeast, mushroom and bread mould. In this mode of nutrition, organisms obtain their food from dead and decaying organic matter. Such organisms are known as saprophytes.

Q. 6 When we observe the lower surface of a leaf through a magnifying lens, we see numerous small openings. Which of the following is the term given to such openings?

(a) Stomata (b) Lamina (c) Mid rib (d) Veins

Ans. ***(a)*** Stomata are the numerous small openings observed on the lower surface of a leaf. Each of these pore is surrounded by a pair of guard cells. The stomata helps in the exchange of gases (CO_2 goes in and O_2 is released out).

Q. 7 Two organisms are good friends and live together. One provides shelter, water and nutrients while the other prepares and provides food. Such an association of organisms is termed as

(a) saprophyte (b) parasite (c) autotroph (d) symbiosis

Ans. ***(d)*** Symbiosis is an association between two different organisms that live together and help each other to survive, e.g. Licher (association between an alga and fungus).

Q. 8 Which of the following raw material is available in the air for photosynthesis?

(a) Oxygen (b) Carbon dioxide
(c) Nitrogen (d) Hydrogen

Ans. ***(b)*** Carbon dioxide is the raw material of photosynthesis that is available in air. It is taken by the plant through the tiny pores, called stomata, present on the surface of leaves.

The other necessary conditions are the presence of water, chlorophyll and sunlight. (Oxygen is released during the process hydrogen comes from water and nitrogen has no role in photosynthesis.)

Very Short Answer Type Questions

Q. 9 Potato and ginger are both underground parts that store food. Where is the food prepared in these plants?

Ans. In both the plants, shoot system and leaves are above ground. They prepare food through photosynthesis and transport it to the underground parts for storage.

Q. 10 Photosynthesis requires chlorophyll and a few other raw materials. Add the missing raw materials to the list given below:
Water, minerals, (a) ...... , (b) ....

Ans. (a) Sunlight (b) Carbon dioxide

Photosynthesis is a process by which green plants make their own food, from CO_2 and H_2O by using sunlight, in the presence of chlorophyll.

Short Answer Type Questions

Q. 11 A goat eats away all the leaves of a small plant (balsam). However, in a few days, new leaves could be seen sprouting in the plant again. How did the plant survive without leaves?

Ans. The plant of balsam survived on the food stored in the stem and roots. It might have undergone gaseous exchange through lenticels on stem.

Q. 12 Unscramble the following to form terms related to modes of nutrition.

(a) RASPAEIT (b) ROPEHYTSAP
(c) TOROPHAUT (d) SIBIOMSYS

Ans. (a) PARASITE (b) SAPROPHYTE
(c) AUTOTROPH (d) SYMBIOSIS

Q. 13 Nitrogen is an essential nutrient for plant growth. But farmers who cultivate pulses as crops like green gram, bengal gram, black gram, etc. do not apply nitrogenous fertilisers during cultivation. Why?

Ans. The plants such as gram, peas, pulses are called **Leguminous plants** (legumes). These plants have root nodules in them which have a symbiotic association with bacteria such as *Rhizobium*. This bacteria convert gaseous nitrogen of air into water soluble nitrogen compounds (like nitrates).

Some of these nitrogen compounds are used by the leguminous plants for their growth. Hence, farmers do not need to apply nitrogenous fertilisers in the fields during cultivation.

Q. 14 Wheat dough if left in the open, after a few days, starts to emit a foul smell and becomes unfit for use. Give reason.

Ans. Carbohydrates in wheat dough encourage the growth of yeast and other saprophytic fungi. They breakdown carbohydrates into simpler compounds like CO_2 and alcohol that leads to a foul smell.

Q. 15 Sunlight, chlorophyll, carbon dioxide, water and minerals are raw materials essential for photosynthesis.

Do you know where they are available? Fill in the blanks with the appropriate raw materials.

(a) Available in the plant : ....
(b) Available in the soil : ....
(c) Available in the air : ....
(d) Available during day : ....

Ans. (a) Available in the plant : **chlorophyll** (Green pigment present in leaves that absorbs energy from sunlight).

(b) Available in the soil : **water and minerals** (These are absorbed by the roots from the soil and are transported to leaves through xylem).

(c) Available in the air : **carbon dioxide** (Enters through the tiny pores called stomata on the surface of leaves).

(d) Available during day : **sunlight** (It is captured by chlorophyll in leaves and is converted into chemical energy).

Q. 16 Observe the given figure and label the following terms given in the box.
Stomatal opening, guard cell

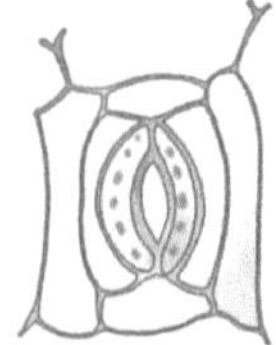

Ans. Labelled figure is given below:

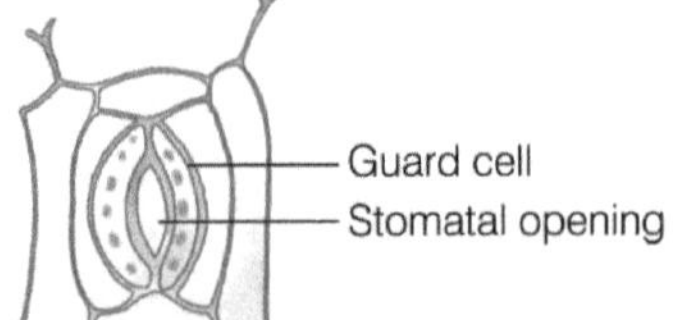

Note *Stomata are the tiny pores for gaseous exchange present on leaf surface. Their opening and closing is controlled by guard cells.*

Long Answer Type Questions

Q. 17 Match the organisms given in column I with their mode of nutrition given in column II.

	Column I		Column II
(a)	Mango tree	(i)	Insectivorous plant
(b)	Mushroom	(ii)	Heterotroph
(c)	Pitcher plant	(iii)	Autotroph
(d)	*Cuscuta*	(iv)	Saprophyte
(e)	Elephant	(v)	Parasitic

Ans. The correct matching is as given:
(a)—(iii), (b)—(iv), (c)—(i), (d)—(v), (e)—(ii)

(a) Mango tree prepares its own food, has green leaves—Autotroph.
(b) Mushroom grows on dead and decaying organic matter and obtain their nutrition from them. So, they are saprophytes.
(c) Pitcher plant has modified leaves that trap insect to obtain nitrogen compounds. Thus, it is an insectivorous plant.
(d) *Cuscuta* does not have chlorophyll. It takes food from the tree on which it climbs, depriving the host tree of nutrients. Therefore, it is parasitic.
(e) Elephant cannot make its own food. So, its a heterotroph.

Q. 18 Wild animals like tiger, wolf, lion and leopard do not eat plants. Does this mean that they can survive without plants? Can you provide a suitable explanation?

Ans. Animals like tiger, wolf, lion and leopard are carnivorous and do not eat plants. They hunt and eat herbivorous animals like deer, gaur, bison, zebra, giraffe, etc., which are dependent on plants for food.

If there are no plants, herbivorous animals will not be able to survive as they will have no food and would die of starvation. This will ultimately affect animals like tiger, wolf, lion and leopard that depend on herbivorous animals for food.

They will have nothing to eat and thus would not survive from this, it can be concluded that all heterotrophs directly or indirectly depend on plants for food and cannot survive without plants.

Q. 19 Fill in the blanks of the paragraph given below with the words provided in box. chlorophyll, energy, food, carbon dioxide, water, photosynthesis

Leaves have a green pigment called ...(a)... which captures ...(b)... from sunlight. This ...(c)... is used in the process of ...(d)... and along with other raw materials like ...(e)... and ...(f)... to synthesise ...(g)... .

Ans. (a) chlorophyll (b) energy (c) energy
(d) photosynthesis (e) carbon dioxide (f) water (g) food

Q. 20 Spot as many organisms as possible in the puzzle given as figure by encircling them as shown. Write the names on a sheet of paper and categorise them into autotrophs and heterotrophs. Classify the heterotrophs into herbivores, carnivores, omnivores and saprophytes.

B	R	O	S	E	A	T	C	R	O	W
A	A	G	N	B	H	I	N	D	I	B
N	B	N	G	I	N	G	E	R	C	L
Y	B	A	N	H	B	E	C	O	W	F
A	I	M	U	S	H	R	O	O	M	F
N	T	G	B	E	R	M	W	F	I	O
E	L	E	P	H	A	N	T	S	C	X
T	S	A	E	Y	N	P	H	B	E	E
C	A	R	R	O	T	U	L	S	I	X

Ans.

B	R	O	S	E	A	T	C	R	O	W
A	A	G	N	B	H	I	N	D	I	B
N	B	N	G	I	N	G	E	R	C	L
Y	B	A	N	H	B	E	C	O	W	F
A	I	M	U	S	H	R	O	O	M	F
N	T	G	B	E	R	M	W	F	I	O
E	L	E	P	H	A	N	T	S	C	X
T	S	A	E	Y	N	P	H	B	E	E
C	A	R	R	O	T	U	L	S	I	X

Autotrophs — Rose, Mango, Bhindi, Carrot, Banyan, Tulsi, Ginger, Yam

Heterotrophs — Elephant, Ant, Yeast, Tiger, Mushroom, Fox, Mice, Owl, Cow, Crow, Rabbit, Bee, Fish

(i) Herbivores — Elephant, Cow, Rabbit, Bee, Ox

(ii) Carnivores — Fox, Tiger

(iii) Omnivores — Ant, Mice, Owl, Crow, Fish

(iv) Saprophytes — Mushroom, Yeast

Q. 21 Can you give me a name?

Solve each of the following riddles by writing the name of the organism and its mode of nutrition. One riddle is solved to help you.

(a) I am tall but I cannot move. I am green and can prepare my own food. <u>tree</u>, <u>autotroph</u>.

(b) I live in water; people keep me in an aquarium and feed me.____,____

(c) I am small and I can fly, I disturb your sleep, bite you and suck your blood which is my food. ____,____

(d) I am white and soft. I grow well in the rainy season. Children pluck me from the ground and admire me. I absorb nutrients from decomposed dead parts of plants and animals in the soil. ______.

Ans. (b) **Fish**, heterotroph

Fish is an aquatic animal. It is kept in aquarium by people. It cannot make its own food. So, its heterotroph.

(c) **Mosquito**, omnivore

A **mosquito** during its life cycle passes through different modes of nutrition. The larvae feeds on microorganisms, the adult female feeds on blood to supply proteins for eggs and adults of both sexes feed on plant nectar. So, it is most appropriate to consider them as an omnivore.

(d) **Mushroom**, saprophyte

Fungi such as mushroom under warm conditions grow on dead parts of plants (e.g. rotting wood of a dead tree) and animals. They obtain nutrition from decaying organic matter. So, they are saprophytes.

2

Nutrition in Animals

Multiple Choice Questions (MCQs)

Q. 1 Given below from (i) to (iv) are some food items.

(i) Boiled and mashed potato
(ii) Glucose solution
(iii) A slice of bread
(iv) Mustard oil

Which of the above will give blue-black colour when tested with iodine?

(a) (i) and (ii)
(b) (i) and (iii)
(c) (ii) and (iii)
(d) (iii) and (iv)

Ans. *(b)* The food containing starch (carbohydrate) on reaction with iodine gives blue-black colour, e.g. Boiled and mashed potato, a slice of bread.
Glucose solution and mustard oil would not give blue-black colour as they are not starch. Mustard oil is fat and glucose is simple unit of carbohydrate.

Q. 2 Which of the following pair of teeth differ in structure but are similar in function?

(a) Canines and incisors
(b) Molars and premolars
(c) Incisors and molars
(d) Premolars and canines

Ans. *(b)* Molars and premolars perform similar function of chewing and grinding the food.
The molars are broader and have different ridge structure than molars.
The other types of teeth are:

- Inciors, chisel-shaped for biting and cutting food.
- Canines, large and pointed for piercing and tearing food.

Q. 3 Read carefully the terms given below. Which of the following set is the correct combination of organs that do not carry out any digestive functions?

(a) Oesophagus, large Intestine, rectum
(b) Buccal cavity, oesophagus, rectum
(c) Buccal cavity, oesophagus, large intestine
(d) Small intestine, large intestine, rectum

Ans. *(a)* In the human digestive system, parts such as oesophagus, large intestine and rectum do not carry out any digestive functions. Oesophagus carries food from the mouth to the stomach.

Large intestine absorbs most of the water from undigested food material. Rectum is the last part of the large intestine where undigested food is stored till it is egested out.

Q. 4 The swallowed food moves downwards in the alimentary canal because of

(a) force provided by the muscular tongue
(b) the flow of water taken with the food
(c) gravitational pull
(d) the contraction of muscles in the wall of foodpipe

Ans. *(d)* As soon as the food enters the food pipe, the muscles in its walls start alternate contractions and relaxation producing a wave-like movement called **peristaltic**. These movements are essential for pushing the food downwards in the alimentary canal.

Q. 5 The acid present in the stomach

(a) kills the harmful bacteria that may enter along with the food
(b) protects the stomach lining from harmful substances
(c) digests starch into simpler sugars
(d) makes the medium alkaline

Ans. *(a)* The inner lining of stomach secretes **mucus**, **hydrochloric acid** and **digestive juices**. out of these HCl kills any bacteria that may enter the stomach with food and makes the medium acidic.

Mucus protects the stomach lining from HCl and digestive juices breakdown proteins in food into simpler substances.

Q. 6 The finger-like outgrowths of *Amoeba* helps to ingest food. However, the finger-like outgrowths of human intestine helps to

(a) digest the fatty food substances
(b) make the food soluble
(c) absorb the digested food
(d) absorb the undigested food

Ans. *(c)* Villi are the finger-like outgrowths of inner surface of human intestine. Their role is to increase the surface area for rapid absorption of digested food.

However, in *Amoeba*, the finger-like projections are called *pseudopoida* that helps it to catch food particles and to move.

Q. 7 Read the following statements with reference to the villi of small intestine.

(i) They have very thin walls.
(ii) They have a network of thin and small blood vessels close to the surface.
(iii) They have small pores through which food can easily pass.
(iv) They are finger-like projections.

Identify those statements which enable the villi to absorb digested food.

Choose the correct option.

(a) (i), (ii) and (iv)
(b) (ii), (iii) and (iv)
(c) (iii) and (iv)
(d) (i) and (iv)

Ans. ***(a)*** The inner surface of small intestine has many finger-like outgrowth called villi to help in absorption of food. They have very thin walls to pass digested nutrients through diffusion. The villi are connected to the blood vessels, so the circulating blood can carry these nutrients away.

Q. 8 The false feet of *Amoeba* are used for

(a) movement only
(b) capture of food only
(c) capture of food and movement
(d) exchange of gases only

Ans. ***(c)*** The false feet or pseudopodia of *Amoeba* are finger-like projections that allow movement (keep on appearing and disappearing as it moves) and help to catch food particles from the surroundings.

Q. 9 The enzymes present in the saliva convert

(a) fats into fatty acids and glycerol
(b) starch into simple sugars
(c) proteins into amino acids
(d) complex sugars into simple sugars

Ans. ***(b)*** The salivary gland present in mouth secretes saliva. It contains the enzyme amylase (ptyalin) that breaks down into simple sugars. Only about 30% starch digestion takes place in the mouth.

Q. 10 Cud is the name given to the food of ruminants which is

(a) swallowed and undigested
(b) swallowed and partially digested
(c) properly chewed and partially digested
(d) properly chewed and completely digested

Ans. ***(b)*** The partially digested food in the rumen (part of stomach) of ruminants (e.g. cow, goat, sheep, etc) is called cud. It is brought back to the mouth in small amounts to be chewed thoroughly.

Q. 11 Choose the correct order of terms that describes the process of nutrition in ruminants.

(a) swallowing → partial digestion → chewing of cud → complete digestion
(b) chewing of cud → swallowing → partial digestion → complete digestion
(c) chewing of cud → swallowing → mixing with digestive juices → digestion
(d) swallowing → chewing and mixing → partial digestion → complete digestion

Ans. ***(a)*** The process of nutrition in ruminants occur as: swallowing → partial digestion (cud) → cud brought back to mouth → chewing of cud → other compartments of stomach → small intestine → complete digestion.

Q. 12 Cellulose rich food substances are good sources of roughage in human beings because

(a) human beings do not have cellulose-digesting enzymes.
(b) cellulose gets absorbed in the human blood and converts into fibres.
(c) the cellulose digesting bacteria convert cellulose into fibres.
(d) cellulose breaks down into smaller components which are egested as roughage.

Ans. ***(a)*** Human beings do not have cellulose digesting enzymes called cellulase but cellulose. is still a very important part of human diet. If forms a major part of roughage that is essential for proper digestion.

Very Short Answer Type Questions

Q. 13 Name the parts of the alimentary canal where

(a) water gets absorbed from undigested food
(b) digested food gets absorbed
(c) taste of the food is perceived
(d) bile juice is produced

Ans. (a) Large intestine (no digestive activity takes place)
(b) Small intestine (numerous villi increase the surface area for absorption)
(c) Tongue (contain taste buds)
(d) Liver (produce bile, that is stored in gall bladder and helps in fats digestion).

Q. 14 Mark the following statements as True or False. If False, write the correct statements.

(a) Tongue is attached to the roof of the mouth cavity at the back.
(b) The large intestine is longer and wider than the small intestine of the human alimentary canal.
(c) Mucus protects the stomach lining from damage.
(d) All heterotrophs have a similar basic process of nutrition.

Ans. (a) False, tongue is attached to the floor of the mouth cavity at the back.
(b) False, the large intestine is smaller and wider than the small intestine of the human alimentary canal.
(c) True.
(d) True.

Q. 15 Choose the odd one out from each group and give reasons.

(a) Liver, salivary gland, starch, gall bladder
(b) Stomach, liver, pancreas, salivary gland
(c) Tongue, absorption, taste, swallow
(d) Oesophagus, small intestine, large intestine, rectum

Ans. (a) Starch is the odd one. It is a type of carbohydrate. All others are parts of digestive system of human.
(b) Stomach is the odd one. It is a digestive organ. All others are glands.
(c) Absorption is the odd one. It is a digestive process that occurs in small intestine. All others are related to mouth.
(d) Small intestine is the odd one. It releases intestinal juices and is involved in digestion. All others do not take part in the digestion process.

Q. 16 You were blindfolded and asked to identify the drinks provided in two different glasses. You could identify drink *A* as lime juice and *B* as bitter gourd juice. How could you do it inspite of being blindfolded?

Ans. Inspite of being blindfolded, one could identify tastes of different drinks with the help of different types of taste buds present in the tongue.

Taste buds are sensory taste receptors that help to or perception of taste.

There are four kinds of taste buds which detect sweet, salty, sour and bitter taste. These are located in different part of the tongue.

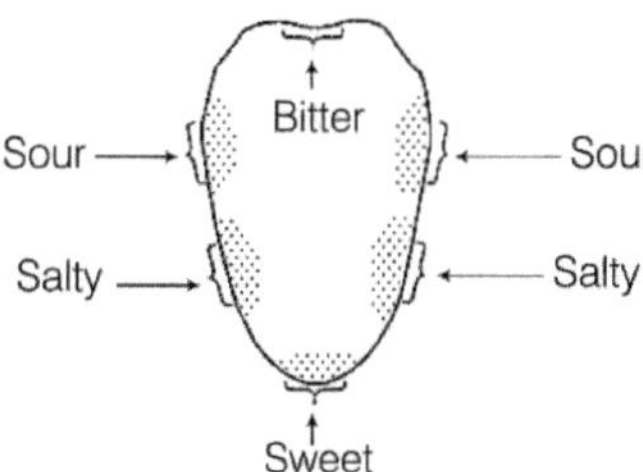

Structure of tongue showing position of taste buds

Q. 17 Fill in the blanks with suitable words:

(a) The alimentary canal stretches from ....to.......... .
(b) Teeth are rooted in separate ....in between the ....
(c) Digestion of food starts in ....and gets completed in ....
(d) ....is the largest gland in the human body.

Ans. (a) mouth; anus (b) sockets; gums
(c) buccal cavity; small intestine. (d) liver

Q. 18 Following statements describe the five steps in animal nutrition. Read each statement and give one word for each statement. Write the terms that describe each process.

(a) Transportation of absorbed food to different parts of body and their utilisation.
(b) Breaking of complex food substances into simpler and soluble substances.
(c) Removal of undigested and unabsorbed solid residues of food from the body.
(d) Taking food into the body.
(e) Transport of digested and soluble food from the intestine to blood vessels.

Ans. (a) Assimilation (b) Digestion (c) Egestion
(d) Ingestion (e) Absorption

Short Answer Type Questions

Q. 19 Match the animals in Column I with their mode of feeding listed in Column II.

Column I (Animals)		Column II (Mode of Feeding)	
(a)	Housefly	(i)	Biting and chewing
(b)	Cockroach	(ii)	Suckling
(c)	Mosquito	(iii)	Sponging
(d)	Infants	(iv)	Sucking

Ans. The correct matching is as given:
(a)—(iii), (b)—(i), (c)—(iv), (d)—(ii)

(a) Housefly is a sponging insect with sponge-like mouth parts that allow them to eat only liquid foods.

(b) Cockroach has primitive arrangement of mouthparts for biting and chewing.

(c) Mosquito has piercing and sucking mouth parts that pierce food items to enable sucking of internal fluids.

(d) Infants suckle milk, as they have no teeth.

Q. 20 Boojho took some grains of boiled rice in test tube '*A*' and Paheli took boiled and chewed rice in test tube '*B*'. Both of them poured 1-2 drops of iodine solution into the test tube and observed the colour change.

What colour change would they have observed? Give reasons for your answer.

Ans. Iodine solution gives a blue-black colour on reacting with starch. In test tube *A*, blue-black colour appeared because starch was present. In test tube *B*, colour of iodine would not change because it contained chewed rice.

Starch in this case has been broken down into simple sugars by the action of amylase present in saliva. The saliva gets mixed with food on chewing.

Q. 21 '*A*' got her gall bladder removed surgically as she was diagnosed with stones in her gall bladder. After the surgery, she faced problems in digestion of certain food items when consumed in bulk. Can you tell which kind of food items would they be and why?

Ans. After surgical removal of gall bladder, '*A*' would face problems in digestion of fatty substances when consumed in bulk.

This is because the bile juice stored in the gall bladder helps in digestion of fats. Removal of gall bladder, thus leads to difficulty in digestion of fatty substances.

Q. 22 Match the organs in Column I with the words listed in Column II.

Column I	Column II
(a) Rectum	(i) Mucus
(b) Gall bladder	(ii) Villi
(c) Stomach	(iii) Taste buds
(d) Tongue	(iv) Faeces
(e) Small intestine	(v) Bile juice

Ans. The correct matching is as given:
(a)—(iv), (b)—(v), (c)—(i), (d)—(iii), (e)—(ii)

Q. 23 Ruminants such as cows and buffaloes swallow their food hurriedly and then sit restfully and chew their food. Can you give reason why?

Ans. Ruminants such as cows and buffaloes swallow their food hurriedly and store it in a part of the stomach called **rumen**. The cellulose of the food is digested here by the action of certain bacteria which are not present in humans.

Later, this partially digested food (cud) is returned to the buccal cavity of the animals in small lumps and animal chews it sitting restfully to complete the process of digestion. This process is called **rumination**.

The thoroughly chewed cud is swallowed again to other compartment of stomach and then into small intestine for complete digestion and absorption.

Q. 24 Boojho and Paheli were eating their food hurriedly so that they could go out and play during the recess. Suddenly, Boojho started coughing violently. Think of the reasons, why he was coughing and discuss with your friends?

Ans. Sometimes, when we eat hurriedly or talk or laugh while eating, the flap-like valve (called epiglottis) which closes the passage of windpipe remains open. Therefore, the food may enter into the windpipe and it leads to coughing. Coughing helps to clear the passage.

Long Answer Type Questions

Q. 25 Fill in the blanks using the words listed below.

Water, front, intestinal, salts, pseudopodia, back, vacuole

(a) The digestion of all food components is completed by the ....juice.

(b) Large intestine absorbs ....and some.........from the undigested food.

(c) Tongue is attached at the .... floor of the mouth cavity and is free at the ....

(d) *Amoeba* pushes out.........around the food and traps it in a food............. .

Ans. (a) intestinal (b) water; salts

(c) back; front (d) pseudopodia; vacuole.

Q. 26 Label the given figure as directed below in *A* to *D* and give the name of each type of teeth.

(i) The cutting and biting teeth as *A*

(ii) The piercing and tearing teeth as *B*

(iii) The grinding and chewing teeth as *C*

(iv) The grinding teeth present only in adults as *D*

Ans. The name of each type of teeth are as given:

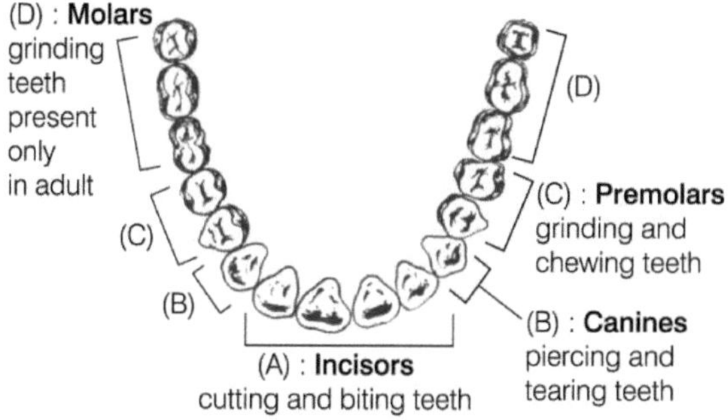

Q. 27 Read the following passage carefully and answer the questions that follow it.

Bile juice is stored in a sac called, gall bladder, located near its organ of secretion, liver. The gall bladder releases the bile juice into the small intestine whenever food reaches there.

Though bile juice is devoid of any digestive enzymes, it is required for the digestion of fats. The fats cannot be digested easily because they are insoluble in water and are present as large globules. Bile juice breaks down big fat droplets into smaller droplets.

These are then easily digested by the enzymes released from the pancreas.

(a) Which organ secretes the bile juice?
(b) Why is digestion of fats difficult as compared to that of other nutrients?
(c) How does bile juice help in digestion of that of other nutrients?
(d) Where is the digestion of fat completed?
(e) Does bile juice digest fat completely?

Ans. (a) Bile juice is secreted by the **liver**.

(b) Digestion of fats is difficult as compared to that of other nutrients because of insolubility of fat in water.

(c) Bile juice helps in digestion of fat by breaking down big fat droplets into smaller droplet. This is called emulsification of fats.

(d) Digestion of fat is completed in **small intestine**.

(e) No, fat is not digested by bile juice. Bile contains bile salts, which helps in its emulsification. This makes the action of pancreatic lipase easier that completes fat digestion.

Q. 28 Label the parts of figure given below and name them.

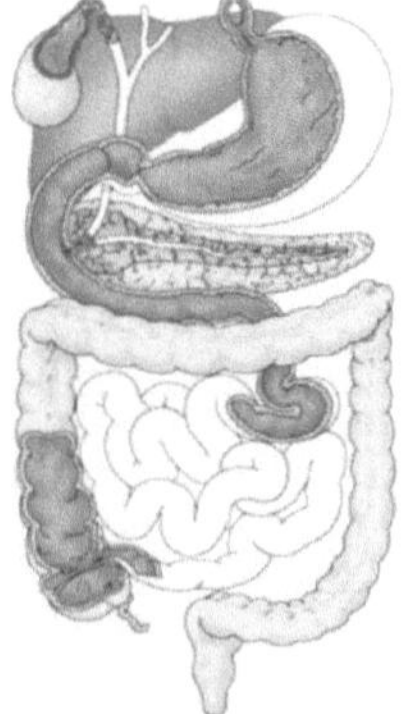

(a) The largest gland in our body.
(b) The organ where protein digestion starts.
(c) The organ that releases digestive juice into the small intestine.
(d) The organ where bile juice gets stored.

Ans. The parts of figure and their name are as given:

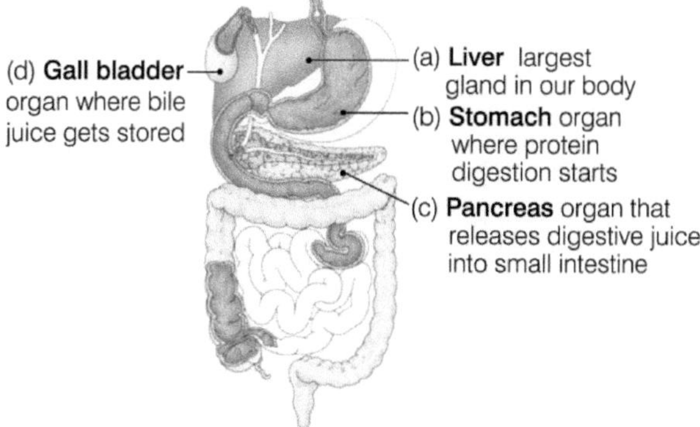

Q. 29 Open your mouth, look into a mirror and try to count the different types of teeth in your mouth. Compare them with figure of question 30. Record your observations in the table below:

Type of teeth	Number of teeth	
	In my mouth	In the figure
Incisors		
Canines		
Premolars		
Molars		

(a) Did you observe any difference in the number of teeth? If yes, could you identify which type of teeth showed the difference?

(b) Compare the number and type of teeth in an adult (say your parents or cousins who have reached the age of 25-30 or more). Note your observation.

Ans.

Type of teeth	Number of teeth	
	In my mouth	In the figure
Incisors	4	4
Canines	2	2
Premolars	4	4
Molars	4	6

(a) Yes, the difference has been observed in the number of molars.

(b) The number and type of teeth vary in an adult as compared to a child. Children have 28 teeth in their mouth.

There are only four molars in each jaw. While, adults have 32 teeth in their mouth which means six molars in each jaw. The third molars, present only in adults are known as wisdom teeth.

Q. 30 Crossword Puzzle

Solve the crossword given as figure.

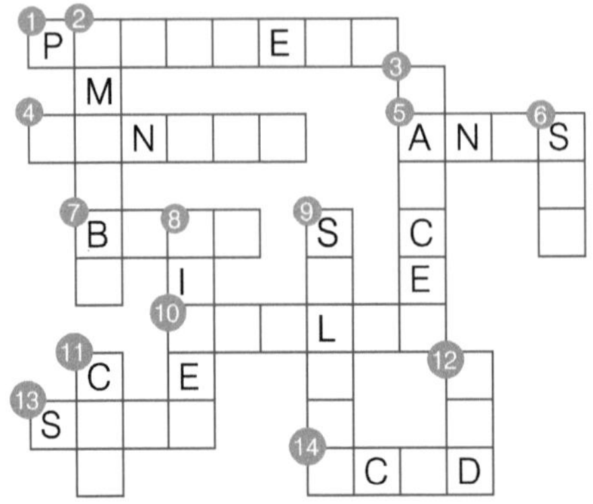

Across

1. Cream coloured digestive gland
4. Organ that mixes saliva with the food
5. Point of defecation
7. Stored in gall bladder
10. Finger-like outgrowth in the small intestine
13. Kind of taste buds
14. Kills bacteria in the stomach

Down

2. Feeds with the help of pseudopodia
3. Undigested excretory solid residues
6. Total number of molars in one jaw of an adult
8. Largest gland
9. Watery secretion in the mouth
11. A ruminant
12. Form of food chewed by ruminants

Ans.

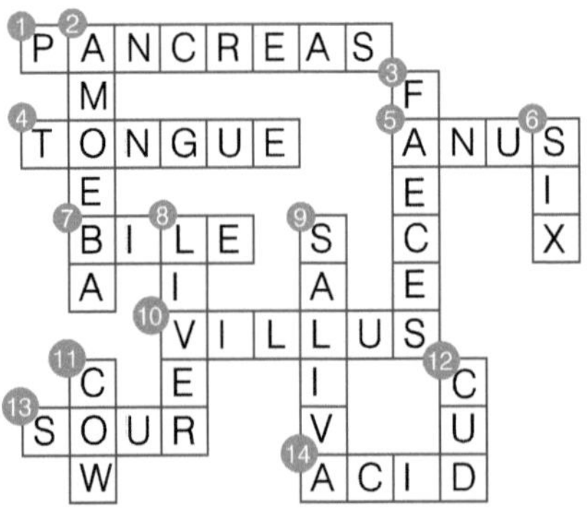

Across

1. PANCREAS
4. TONGUE
5. ANUS
7. BILE
10. VILLUS
13. SOUR
14. ACID

Down

2. *AMOEBA*
3. FAECES
6. SIX
8. LIVER
9. SALIVA
11. COW
12. CUD

3

Fibre to Fabric

Multiple Choice Questions (MCQs)

Q. 1 The rearing of silkworms for obtaining silk is called

(a) cocoon (b) silk
(c) sericulture (d) silviculture

Ans. *(c)* Sericulture is a practice of rearing silkworms for obtaining silk while silviculture is a practice of developing and caring forests.

Q. 2 Which of the following is not a type of silk?

(a) Mulberry silk (b) Tassar silk
(c) Mooga silk (d) Moth silk

Ans. *(d)* Moth is the silkworm under development inside a cocoon. Mulberry, Tassar and Mooga are varieties of silk produced by different rearing practices.

Q. 3 Paheli wanted to buy a gift made of animal fibre obtained without killing the animal. Which of the following would be the right gift for her to buy?

(a) Woollen shawl (b) Silk scarf
(c) Animal fur cap (d) Leather jacket

Ans. *(a)* Rest of the options given here are obtained by killing animals, but wool is produced from shearing of skin of sheep.

Q. 4 Silk fibre is obtained from

(a) fleece of sheep (b) cotton ball
(c) cocoon (d) shiny jute stalk

Ans. *(c)* Cocoon is one of the stage of life cycle of silkworm. Fleece of sheep gives wool, cotton ball gives cotton and jute stalk gives jute fibre.

Q. 5 Wool fibre cannot be obtained from which of the following?

(a) Goat (b) Llama
(c) Alpaca (d) Moth

Ans. *(d)* Moth is an insect while other three are the animals with fur which produce wool.

Q. 6 Selective breeding is a process of

(a) selecting the offsprings with desired properties
(b) selecting the parents with desired properties
(c) selecting an area for breeding
(d) selecting fine hair for good quality wool

Ans. *(b)* When certain desired traits (properties) of parents are considered before breeding, it is called selective breeding.

Q. 7 The general process that takes place at a sheep shearing shed is

(a) removal of fleece
(b) separating hair of different textures
(c) washing of sheep fibre to remove grease
(d) rolling of sheep fibre into yarn

Ans. *(a)* Removal of fleece is called sheep shearing, separating hair of different textures is called sorting, washing wool to remove grease is called scouring and rolling of sheep fibre into yarn is called rolling.

Q. 8 The term sericulture is used for

(a) culture of bacteria (b) rearing of silkworm
(c) making silk fabric from silk yarn (d) production of sarees

Ans. *(b)* Sericulture is the rearing of silkworm to obtain silk fibre. Sericulture means 'silk farming'.

Q. 9 Reeling of silk is

(a) a process of making silk reels
(b) spinning of silk fibres
(c) weaving of silk cloth
(d) the process of taking silk threads from cocoon

Ans. *(d)* Reeling of silk is the process of taking out threads from the cocoon for use as silk.

Q. 10 Silkworms secrete fibre made of

(a) fat (b) cellulose (c) protein (d) nylon

Ans. *(c)* Silk protein consists of sericin and fibroin mainly. Fat and cellulose are not present in silk. Nylon is a synthetic fibre.

Very Short Answer Type Questions

Q. 11 Fill in the blanks in the following statements.

(a) ________ and ________ fibres are obtained from animals.
(b) Silk fibres come from ________ of silk ________ .
(c) Wool yielding animals bear ________ on their body.
(d) Hair trap a lot of ________ which is a poor ________ of heat.

Ans. (a) Silk, wool (b) cocoon, worm
(c) fleece (hair) (d) air, conductor

Q. 12. State whether the following statements are True or False. If false, correct them.

(a) Silkworms are caterpillars of silk moth.
(b) In India, camels and goats are generally reared for obtaining wool.
(c) The rearing of silkworms for obtaining silk is called silviculture.
(d) In the process of obtaining wool from fleece, sorting is done after scouring.
(e) Yak hair are not used to make woollen fabric.

Ans. (a) True
(b) False, sheep are mostly reared for wool in India.
(c) False, it is called sericulture, silviculture is caring and developing forests.
(d) True
(e) False, wool can be made from sheep, yak, llama, camel, alpaca and goats.

Q. 13 How do the hair of certain animals help in keeping their bodies warm?

Ans. Hair (or wool) of these animals trap a lot of air. Air is a poor conductor of heat. So, the air trapped in hair (or wool) of these animals prevents their body heat from being lost to cold surroundings and keeps them warm.

Short Answer Type Questions

Q. 14 Match the items of Column I with the items given in Column II.

	Column I		Column II
(a)	Yak wool	(i)	Sheared hair
(b)	Angora goats	(ii)	Silkworm
(c)	Mulberry leaves	(iii)	Tibet and Ladakh
(d)	Scouring	(iv)	Jammu and Kashmir

Ans. The correct matching is as given
(a)—(iii), (b)—(iv), (c)—(ii), (d)—(i)

Note *Yak are found in Tibet and Ladakh, while angora goats are reared in Jammu and Kashmir. Mulberry leaves are used to feed silkworm. Scouring is the process to clean sheared hair.*

Q. 15 Various steps involved to obtain wool from fleece are given here.

(i) Picking out the burrs
(ii) Dyeing in various colours
(iii) Shearing
(iv) Scouring
(v) Sorting

Write the above steps in the correct sequence in which they are carried out.

Ans. The correct sequence is
Shearing → Scouring → Sorting → Picking out the burrs → Dyeing in various colours

Q. 16 Some words related with silk are jumbled up. Write them in their correct form.

(a) TURECULRISE (b) WILSMORK
(c) BELMURRY (d) RINGLEE

Ans. (a) SERICULTURE (b) SILKWORM (c) MULBERRY (d) REELING

Q. 17 Figure shows three rings of circles with letters in them. Some of these letters in each ring can form the name of one wool yielding animal. Find the names of these animals.

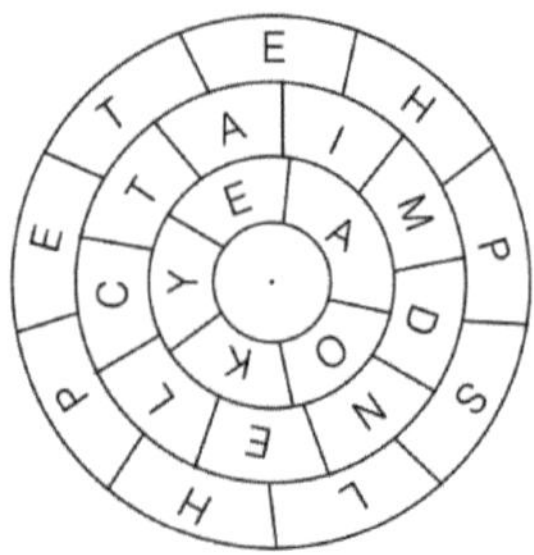

Ans. These animals are yak, camel and sheep.

Q. 18 Write a caption for each of the figure given as figure (a-d).

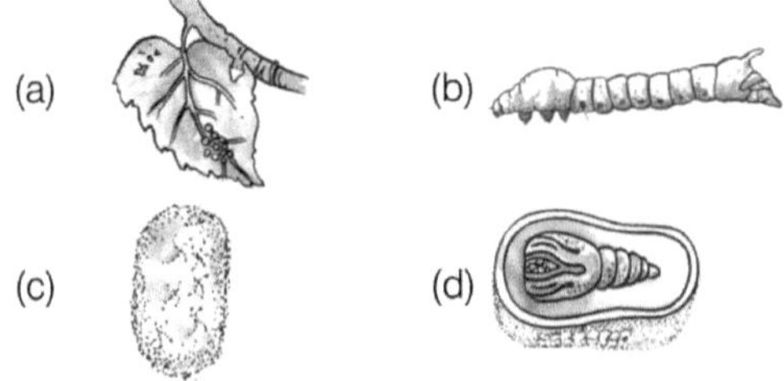

Ans. (a) Eggs of silk moth on mulberry leaf
(b) Silkworm
(c) Cocoon
(d) Cocoon with developing moth

Q. 19 Steps for the production of silk are given below in a jumbled order. Arrange them in their proper sequence.

(a) Eggs are warmed to a suitable temperature for the larvae to hatch from eggs.
(b) Fibres are taken out from the cocoon.
(c) After 25 to 30 days, the caterpillars stop eating and start spinning cocoons.
(d) The larvae/caterpillars or silkworms are kept in clean trays along with freshly chopped mulberry leaves.
(e) Female silk moths lay eggs.
(f) Cocoons are kept under the sun or boiled in water.

Ans. The correct order is

(e) Female silk moths lay eggs.

(a) Eggs are warmed to a suitable temperature for the larvae to hatch from eggs.

(d) The larvae/caterpillars or silkworms are kept in clean trays along with freshly chopped mulberry leaves.

(c) After 25 to 30 days, the caterpillars stop eating and start spinning cocoons.

(f) Cocoons are kept under the sun or boiled in water.

(b) Fibres are taken out from the cocoon.

Q. 20 A wholesale woollen fibre dealer gets the woollen fibre of different textures sorted for various purposes. Match the items in Column I with the woollen fibre in Column II.

	Column I		Column II
(a)	Pashmina shawl	(i)	Camel wool
(b)	Woollen carpet	(ii)	Angora wool
(c)	Baby blanket	(iii)	Kashmiri goat
(d)	Woollen sweater	(iv)	Sheep wool

Ans. The correct matching is as given

(a)—(iii), (b)—(i), (c)—(ii), (d)—(iv)

Long Answer Type Questions

Q. 21 Complete the paragraph related to the life history of silk moth by filling in the blanks.

The (a)...... silk moth lays (b)...... from which hatch (c)...... called (d)...... or (e)...... . They grow in size and when the caterpillar is ready to enter the next stage of its life history called (f)...... . It first weaves a covering to hold itself which is known as (g)...... .

Ans. (a) female (b) eggs (c) larvae

(d) caterpillars (e) silkworm (f) pupa

(g) cocoon

Q. 22 Paheli went to the market to buy sarees for her mother. She took out a thread from the edge of the two sarees shown by the shopkeeper and burnt them. One thread burnt with a smell of burning hair and the other burnt with the smell of burning paper. Which thread is from a pure cotton saree and which one from a pure silk saree? Give reason for your answer.

Ans. In first saree, one thread which burnt with a smell of burning hair is from pure silk, silk and hair are protein fibres. So, on burning these threads, a smell of burning hair comes out. In second saree, second thread which burnt with the smell of burning paper is from a cotton saree.

Since, cotton and paper both are carbohydrates and on burning, they give similar smell.

Q. 23 Explain the phrase – 'Unity is Strength' on the basis of the making of fabric from fibre.

Ans. Fibres and fabric play a large role in everyday applications. A fibre is a hair-like strand of material. They are the smallest visible unit of a fabric and denoted by being extremely long in relation to their width. Fibres can be spun into yarn and made into fabric.

A single fibre is too weak to break but when some fibres together make a fabric, it is difficult to tear. Fabric needs more energy to tear apart as compared to a single fibre.

Q. 24 Write various steps for processing fibres into wool.

Ans. The various steps for processing fibres into wool are as follows:

(i) **Shearing** The first step is to remove fleece of the sheep along with thin layer of skin. This process is called shearing.

(ii) **Scouring** In this step, the sheared hair is washed thoroughly to remove grease, dust and dirt.

(iii) **Sorting** In this step, different textures of hair are separated or sorted.

(iv) **Separating burrs** Burrs are small fluffy fibres which are picked out from the hair.

(v) **Dyeing** The fibres are dyed in various colours, as the original colours of fleece are usually black, white or brown.

(vi) **Rolling** In this process, the fibres are straightened, combed and rolled into yarn. And the fibres now as wool are ready to be woven.

Q. 25 Describe the life history of silk moth with the help of figures of various stages.

Ans. The life cycle of silk moth is completed in four main stages as depicted below in the diagram:

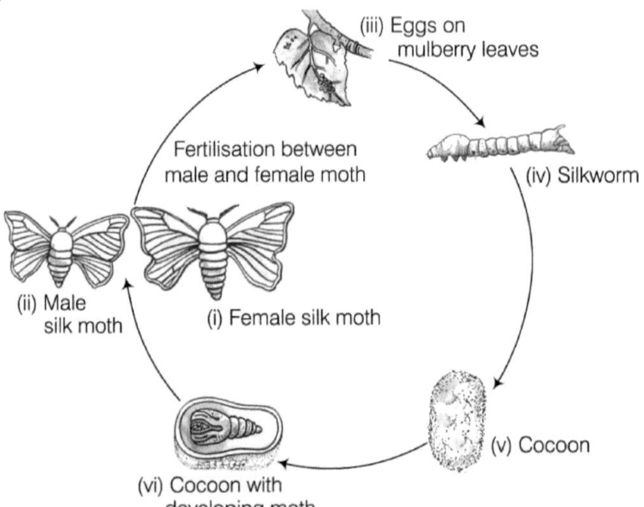

The female silk moth lays eggs on the leaves of a mulberry tree. The eggs hatch to form larvae called 'caterpillar' or 'silkworms'. The silkworms grow in size feeding on mulberry leaves and when the caterpillar is ready to enter the next stage of its life history called pupa, it first weaves a covering to hold itself, which is known as cocoon.

Pupa develop inside cocoon into moth and comes out as an adult male or female silk moth.

4

Heat

Multiple Choice Questions (MCQs)

Q. 1 A marble tile would feel cold as compared to a wooden tile on a winter morning because the marble tile

(a) is a better conductor of heat than the wooden tile

(b) is polished while wooden tile is not polished

(c) reflects more heat than wooden tile

(d) is a poor conductor of heat than the wooden tile

Ans. *(a)* Since, a marble tile is a good conductor of heat as compared to the wood, therefore a marble tile will allow heat to pass through itself easily, keeping it cool on a winter morning.

Q. 2 A beggar wrapped himself with a few layers of newspaper on a cold winter night. This helped him to keep himself warm because

(a) friction between the layers of newspaper produces heat

(b) air trapped between the layers of newspaper is a bad conductor of heat

(c) newspaper is a conductor of heat

(d) newspaper is at a higher temperature than the temperature of the surroundings

Ans. *(b)* The air trapped between the layers of newspaper does not allow heat to pass through, so it helps the beggar to keep himself warm.

Q. 3 Paheli and Boojho measured their body temperatures. Paheli found her's to be 98.6°F and Boojho recorded 37°C. Which of the following statement is true?

(a) Paheli has a higher body temperature than Boojho

(b) Paheli has a lower body temperature than Boojho

(c) Both have normal body temperature

(d) Both are suffering from fever

Ans. *(c)* The temperature 37°C is described in celsius scale while the temperature 98.6°F is described in Fahrenheit scale but they are actually equal. Both these values represent the normal average temperature of a human body.

Q. 4 Boojho has three thermometers as shown in figure. He wants to measure the temperature of his body and that of boiling water. Which thermometer(s) should he choose?

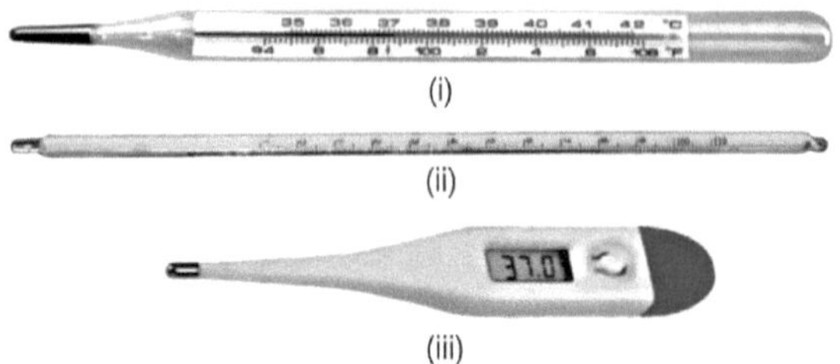

(i)

(ii)

(iii)

(a) Thermometers (i) and (iii) for measuring body temperature and (ii) for measuring the temperature of boiling water
(b) Thermometer (i) for measuring temperature of both
(c) Thermometer (ii) for measuring temperature of both
(d) Thermometer (iii) for measuring temperature of both

Ans. ***(a)*** Thermometers (i) and (iii) are clinical thermometers used to measure body temperature and (ii) is laboratory thermometer used to measure the temperature of boiling water or any object other than human body.

Q. 5 Four arrangements to measure temperature of ice in beaker with laboratory thermometer are shown in figure (a, b, c, d). Which one of them shows the correct arrangement for accurate measurement of temperature?

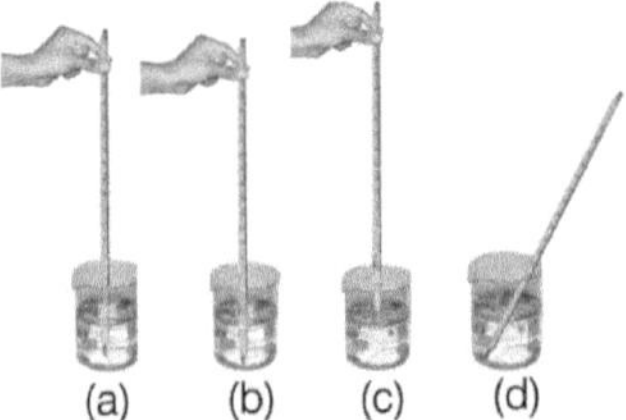

(a) (b) (c) (d)

Ans. ***(a)*** The correct arrangement is shown in figure (a). For accurate measurement of temperature, a laboratory thermometer must be kept upright not tilted and the bulb should be completely surrounded by the substance of which the temperature is to be measured. Also, the bulb should not touch the surface of the container.

Q. 6 Figure (a, b, c, d) shows a student reading a doctor's thermometer. Which of the figure indicates the correct method of reading temperature?

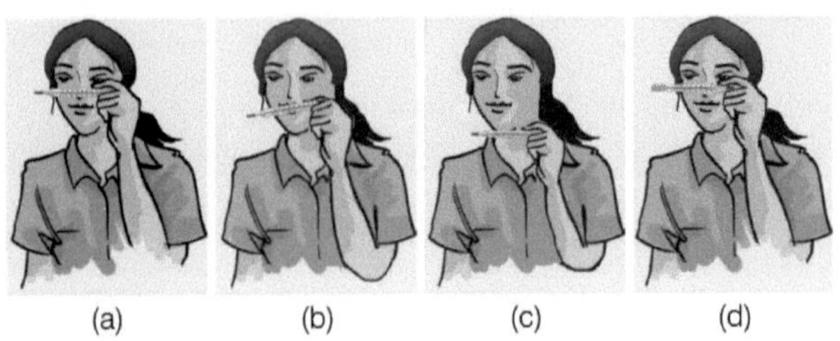

(a) (b) (c) (d)

Ans. ***(a)*** In first case, eyes of student are in level of mercury in thermometer, so it is the correct way to read the temperature in a clinical thermometer.

Q. 7 Figure (a, b, c, d) shows the readings of four different thermometers. Indicate which of the reading shows the normal human body temperature?

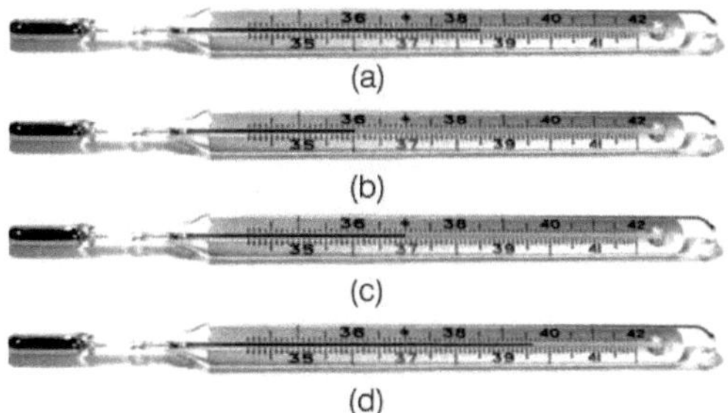

Ans. ***(c)*** As we know that normal body temperature is 37°C. So, the correct option is (c).

Very Short Answer Type Questions

Q. 8 Shopkeepers selling ice blocks usually cover them with jute sacks. Explain why.

Ans. Since, a jute sack is a thermal insulator, therefore, it helps ice not to melt immediately. So, shopkeepers must use insulating materials like sack, saw dust, newspaper etc, to cover the ice.

Q. 9 A laboratory thermometer *A* is kept 7 cm away on the side of the flame while a similar thermometer *B* is kept 7 cm above the flame of a candle as shown in figure. Which of the thermometers *A* or *B*, will show a greater rise in temperature? Give reason for your answer.

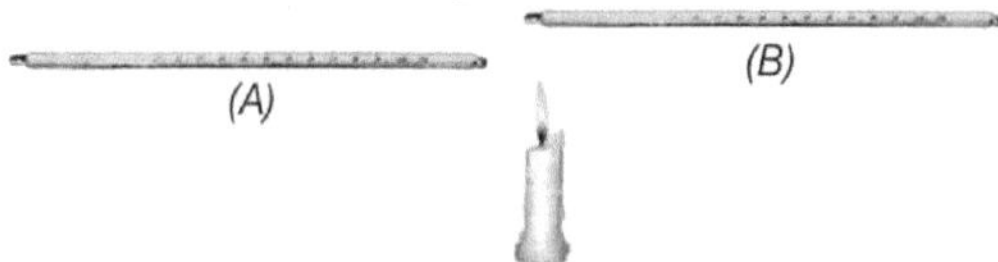

Ans. Thermometer *B* whose bulb is just above the candle flame, will show a greater rise in temperature because hot air above the candle rises up immediately and increases the temperature of bulb of thermometer *B* higher than that of *A*.

Q. 10 To keep her soup warm, Paheli wrapped the container, in which it was kept a woollen cloth. Can she apply the same method to keep a glass of cold drink cool? Give reason for your answer.

Ans. Yes, she can apply the same method to keep a glass of cold drink cool because wool is a thermal insulator, and it cannot allow heat to pass through it.

Q. 11 In a mercury thermometer, the level of mercury rises when its bulb comes in contact with a hot object. What is the reason for this rise in the level of mercury?

Ans. As the temperature increases, expansion of mercury takes place in the capillary tube which leads to the rise in the level of mercury in thermometer.

Short Answer Type Questions

Q. 12 A circular metal loop is heated at point *O* as shown in figure.

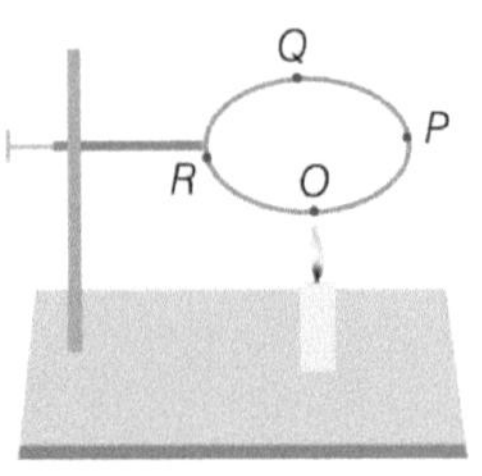

(a) In which direction, would heat flow in the loop?

(b) In which order, the pins at points *P*, *Q* and *R* fixed with the help of wax fall if points *O*, *P*, *Q* and *R* are equidistant from each other?

Ans. (a) Heat will flow in both the directions i.e. from *O* to *P* and *O* to *R*.

(b) First of all pins at *P* and *R* will fall simultaneously and after that pin at *Q* will fall because equal amount of heat will reach the pins at *P* and *R* first.

Q. 13 In the arrangements *A* and *B* as shown in figure, pins *P* and *Q* are fixed to a metal loop and an iron rod with the help of wax. In which case are both the pins likely to fall at different times? Explain.

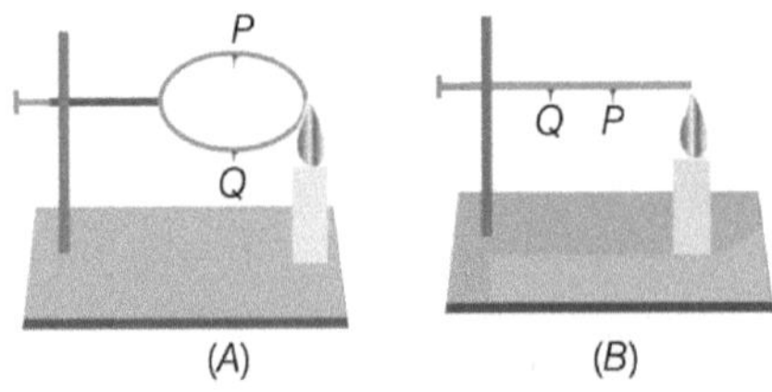

Ans. As from the given figures *A* and *B*, in case of *A*, pins at *P* and *Q* get equal amount of heat, so pins fixed at *P* and *Q* in case of *A* will fall simultaneously.

But in case of *B* pin at point *P* falls before the pin at *Q* as because heat will reach the pin at *P* first than the pin at *Q*.

Q. 14 For setting curd, a small amount of curd is added to warm milk. The microbes present in the curd help in setting if the temperature of the mixture remains approximately between 35°C to 40°C. At places where room temperature remains much below the range, setting of curd becomes difficult. Suggest a way to set curd in such a situation.

Ans. For the setting of curd at places where temperature is below room temperature, the container in which curd is to be made, must be kept in a thermally insulated cover or it can be wrapped either by a woollen material or a jute sack so that temperature is maintained for the setting of curd.

The container can also be kept in the sun or near the gas stove while cooking food for the setting of curd.

Q. 15 You may have noticed that a few sharp jerks are given to clinical thermometer before using it. Why is it done so?

Ans. Jerks are given to clinical thermometer before using it to settle down the mercury level below normal temperature so that the measurement of temperature of a body can be taken accurately.

Q. 16 It is advised not to hold the thermometer by its bulb while reading it. Explain, why.

Ans. We are advised not to hold the thermometer bulb while reading it, as the level of mercury increases from the actual reading due to our body temperature.

Q. 17 At a camp site there are tents of two shades. One made with black fabric and the other with white fabric. Which one will you prefer for resting on a hot summer afternoon? Give reason for your choice. Would you like to prefer the same tent during winter?

Ans. We will prefer a white fabric tent in case of summer because it reflects all the radiations from the sun and keeps us cool inside the tent.
No, in case of winter, we should use a black fabric tent as it absorbs all colours of light from the sun and keeps us warm inside the tent.

Q. 18 While constructing a house in a coastal area, in which direction should the windows preferably face and why?

Ans. Windows should preferably face towards the sea beach because the sea breeze coming from sea keeps the house cool during the day time.

Q. 19 Observe the picture given in figure. Water is being boiled in a pan of wide base.

(a) Which position *P* or *T* will feel warmer?

(b) Fill up the boxes *P* and *T* to indicate the mode of flow of heat to the hand.

Ans. (a) From the given diagram, position *P* will feel warmer because of hot air rising up.

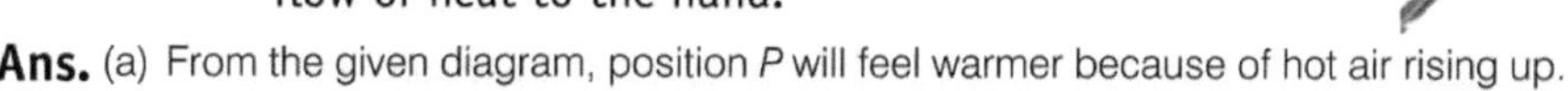

(b) The flow of heat to *P* is a convection process because the air near the boiling water gets hot and rises. However, on the sides such as at *T*, there is no convection and air does not feel as hot as at the top. Therefore, flow of heat to *T* is a radiation process.

Q. 20 Look at figure

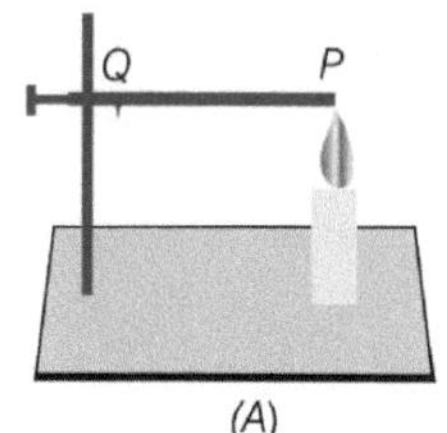

(A)

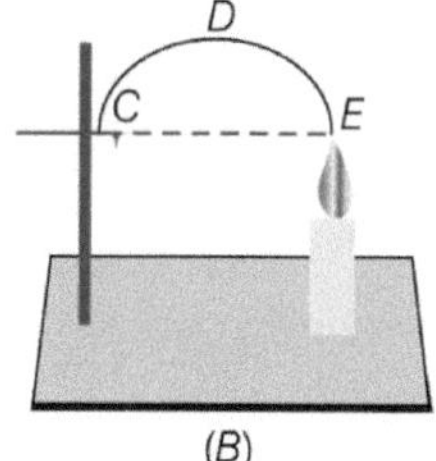

(B)

The length of wire *PQ* in case of *A* is equal to the diameter of the semicircle formed by the wire *CDE*, in case *B*. One pin is attached to each wire with the help of wax as shown in figure. Which pin will fall first? Explain.

Ans. The pin on the wire *PQ* in case *A* will fall first because the heat will reach to the pin on straight wire *PQ* before the heat reaches the pin on the semicircular wire *CDE* in case *B*.

5

Acids, Bases and Salts

Multiple Choice Questions (MCQs)

Q. 1 The correct way of making a solution of acid in water is to

(a) add water to acid
(b) add acid to water
(c) mix acid and water simultaneously
(d) add water to acid in a shallow container

Ans. *(b)* Making solution of acid and water evolve heat. Acid should be added to water dropwise.

Q. 2 Products of a neutralisation reaction are always

(a) an acid and a base
(b) an acid and a salt
(c) a salt and water
(d) a salt and a base

Ans. *(c)* Acid and base participate in neutralisation reaction and produce salt and water.

Q. 3 Turmeric is a natural indicator. On adding its paste to acid and base separately, which colours would be observed?

(a) Yellow in both acid and base
(b) Yellow in acid and red in base
(c) Pink in acid and yellow in base
(d) Red in acid and blue in base

Ans. *(b)* Turmeric paste is yellow in acidic solution and turns red in basic solution.

Q. 4 Phenolphthalein is a synthetic indicator and its colours in acidic and basic solutions respectively are

(a) red and blue
(b) blue and red
(c) pink and colourless
(d) colourless and pink

Ans. *(d)* Phenolphthalein remains colourless in acidic solution but turns pink in basic solution.

Q. 5 When the soil is too basic, plants do not grow well in it. To improve its quality, what must be added to the soil?

(a) Organic matter (b) Quicklime (c) Slaked lime (d) Calamine solution

Ans. *(a)* Organic matter (called manure or compost) releases acids which neutralise the excess bases present in the soil and reduce its basic nature.

Q. 6 'Litmus' a natural dye in an extract of which of the following

(a) China rose (Gudhal) (b) Beetroot
(c) Lichen (d) Blue berries (Jamun)

Ans. *(c)* Litmus is a mauve (purple) colour pigment obtained from Lichens. It turns red when added to acidic solution and blue when added to a basic solution.

Q. 7 Neutralisation reaction is a

(a) physical and reversible change (b) physical change that cannot be reversed
(c) chemical and reversible change (d) chemical change that cannot be reversed

Ans. *(d)* Neutralisation reaction is a chemical reaction between acid and base to produce salt and water. It cannot be reversed.

Q. 8 A solution changes the colour of turmeric indicator from yellow to red. The solution is

(a) basic (b) acidic (c) neutral (d) None of these

Ans. *(a)* Basic solution changes the turmeric indicator from yellow to red.

Q. 9 Which of the following sets of substances contains acids?

(a) Grapes, lime water (b) Vinegar, soap
(c) Curd, milk of magnesia (d) Curd, vinegar

Ans. *(d)* Curd contains lactic acid and vinegar contains acetic acid. Lime water, soap and milk of magnesia are basic substances and grapes contains tartaric acid.

Q. 10 On adding phenolphathalein indicator to a colourless solution, no change is observed. What is the nature of this solution?

(a) Basic (b) Either acidic or basic
(c) Either acidic or neutral (d) Either basic or neutral

Ans. *(c)* Phenophthalein is colourless in acidic and neutral medium but turns pink when introduced in basic medium.

Q. 11 Which of the following is an acid-base indicator?

(a) Vinegar (b) Lime water (c) Turmeric (d) Baking soda

Ans. *(c)* Turmeric paste changes it colour from yellow to red when treated with a base. So, turmeric is an acid-base indicator.

Very Short Answer Type Questions

Q. 12 Look at the given reaction, Hydrochloric acid + Sodium hydroxide (base) → Sodium chloride (salt) + Water; Sodium chloride formed in this reaction remains in solution form. Can we get solid sodium chloride from this solution? Suggest a method (if any).

Ans. We can get solid sodium chloride by evaporation method. Water changes to vapour form during evaporation and solid sodium chloride is left in the container.

Q. 13 State whether the following statements are true or false. Correct the false statements.

(a) All substances are either acidic or basic.
(b) A compound if acidic will turn all indicators red.
(c) Lime water turns red litmus blue.
(d) Common salt dissolved in water turns blue litmus red.
(e) Phenolphthalein is a natural indicator.
(f) Calamine can be used to treat ant's sting.
(g) Lemon water is basic in nature.

Ans. (a) False, some substances, are neutral like water, table salt etc.

(b) False, acids do not turn all indicators red, e.g. China rose indicator turns to dark pink (magenta) when acidic compound is added to it.

(c) True, lime water is basic.

(d) False, common salt and water both are neutral hence, have no effect on litmus.

(e) False, phenolphthalein is synthetic indicator.

(f) True, calamine is basic in nature, while ant's sting is acidic. Thus, calamine causes relief from the sting.

(g) False, lemon water is acidic in nature.

Q. 14 Paheli is suffering from indigestion due to acidity. Is it advisable to give her orange juice in this situation and why?

Ans. No, because orange juice is acidic in nature. Instead she should be given an antacid (milk of magnesia), which is base and neutralise the acidity. Milk of magnesia contains a base magnesium hydroxide which reacts with the acid and cures indigestion.

Short Answer Type Questions

Q. 15 Look at the figure which shows solutions taken in test tubes *A, B, C* and *D*. What colour is expected, when a piece of red litmus paper is dropped in each test tube? Nature of the solutions is given in the table for your help.

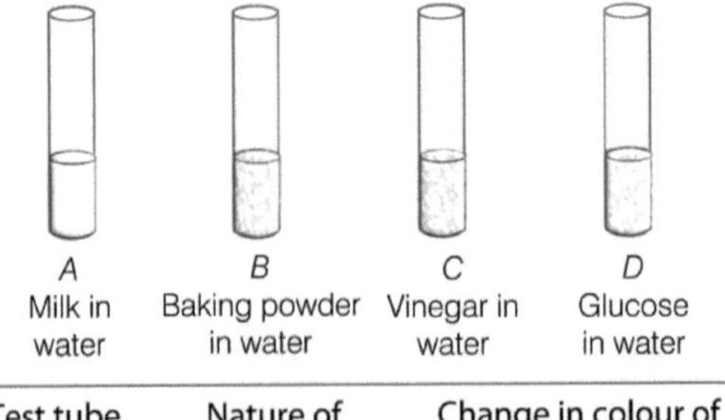

Test tube	Nature of solution	Change in colour of red litmus
A	Neutral	
B	Basic	
C	Acidic	
D	Neutral	

Ans. Change in colour of red litmus is given below:

Test tube	Nature of solution	Change in colour of red litmus
A	Neutral	No change
B	Basic	Turn blue
C	Acidic	No change
D	Neutral	No change

Q. 16 While playing in a park, a child was stung by a wasp. Some elders suggested applying paste of baking soda and others lemon juice as remedy. Which remedy do you think is appropriate and why?

Ans. Wasp sting inject a liquid in the skin which is acidic in nature. Hence, baking soda is the appropriate remedy as it is basic in nature and neutralises the acid.

Q. 17 Form a sentence using the following words :
baking soda, ant bite, moist, effect, neutralised, rubbing

Ans. The effect of an ant bite can be neutralised by rubbing moist baking soda.

Q. 17 Match the substances in Column I with those in Column II.

	Column I		Column II
(a)	Tartaric acid	(i)	Soap
(b)	Calcium hydroxide	(ii)	Curd
(c)	Formic acid	(iii)	Unripe mangoes
(d)	Sodium hydroxide	(iv)	Ant's sting
(e)	Lactic acid	(v)	Lime water

Ans. The correct matching is as given
(a)—(iii), (b)—(v), (c)—(iv), (d)—(i), (e)—(ii)

Q. 19 Fill in the blanks.

a. Lemon juice and vinegar taste .... because they contain ....
b. Turmeric and litmus are .... acid-base indicators.
c. Phenolphthalein gives .... colour with lime water.
d. When an acidic solution is mixed with a basic solution, they .... each other forming .... and water.

Ans. (a) sour, acids

(b) natural

(c) pink
Note *Lime water is basic.*

(d) neutralise, salt
Note *This reaction is called neutralisation reaction.*

Long Answer Type Questions

Q. 20 Boojho, Paheli and their friend Golu were provided with a test tube, each containing China rose solution which was pink in colour. Boojho added 2 drops of solution *'A'* in his test tube and got dark pink colour. Paheli added 2 drops of solution *'B'* to her test tube and got green colour. Golu added 2 drops of solution *'C'* but could not get any change in colour. Suggest the possible cause for the variation in their results.

Ans. China rose (gudhal) is an acid-base indicator.

China rose solution in different medium shows following changes:

China rose + acid ⟶ give dark pink colour, hence *A* is an acidic solution.

China rose + base ⟶ give green colour, hence *B* is a basic solution.

China rose + neutral ⟶ no change in colour, hence *C* is a neutral solution.

Q. 21 Crossword Puzzle

Fill in the crossword given as figure with the help of the clues provided.

Across

2. The solution which does not change the colour of either red or blue litmus.
4. Phenolphthalein gives pink colour in this type of solution.
7. Colour of blue litmus in lemon juice.

Down

1. It is used to test whether a substance is acidic or basic.
3. It is a natural indicator and gives pink colour in basic solution.
5. Nature of ant's sting.
6. It is responsible for increase in temperature during a neutralisation reaction.

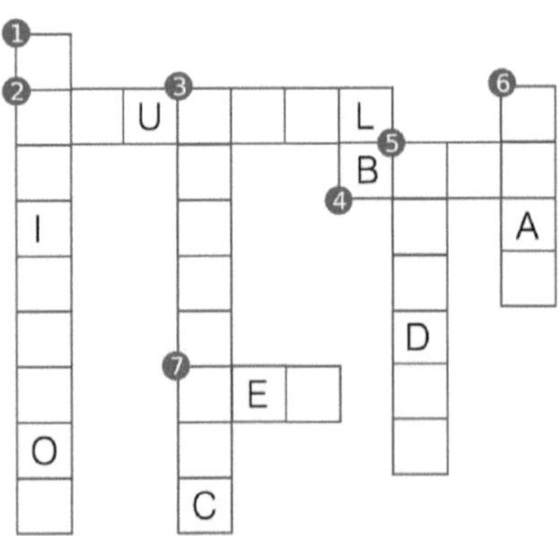

Ans. **Across**

2. NEUTRAL
4. BASE
7. RED

Down

1. INDICATOR
3. TURMERIC
5. ACIDIC
6. HEAT

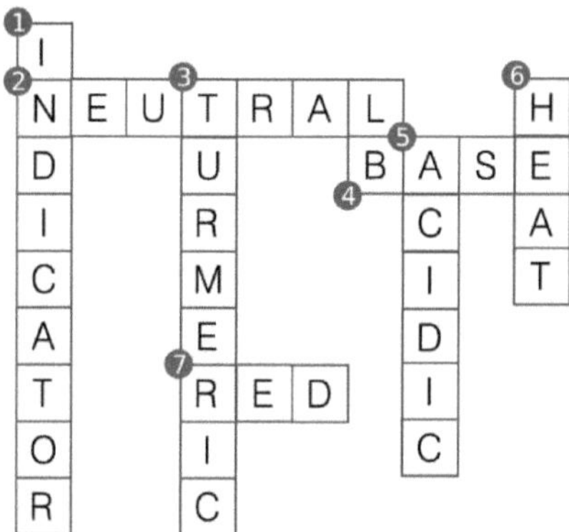

Q. 22 **A farmer was unhappy because of his low crop yield. He discussed the problem with an agricultural scientist and realised that the soil of his field was either too acidic or too basic. What remedy would you suggest the farmer to neutralise the soil?**

Ans. The soil may be acidic or basic naturally. The excessive use of fertilisers in the fields also makes the soil too acidic. When the soil is too acidic, it is treated with base such as quicklime (calcium oxide) or slaked lime (calcium hydroxide) which neutralises the excess acid present in the soil and reduces its acidic nature.

If the soil is too basic, then decaying organic matter (called manure or compost) is added it. The decaying organic matter releases acid which neutralises the excess bases present in the soil and reduces its basic nature.

Q. 23 **You are provided with four test tubes containing sugar solution, baking soda solution, tamarind solution, salt solution. Write down an activity to find the nature (acidic/basic/neutral) of each solution.**

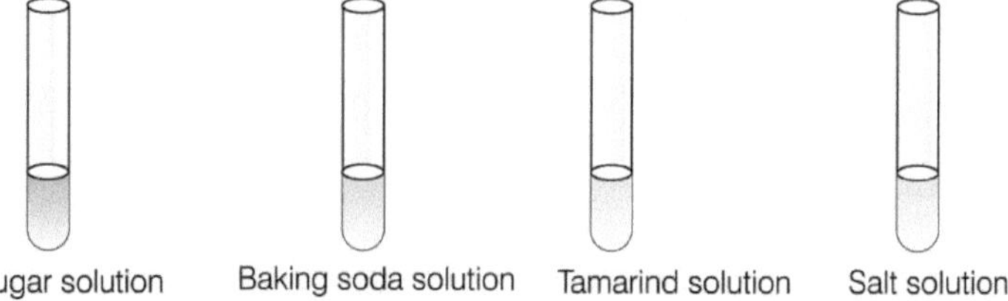

Ans. We can use both red and blue litmus solutions to find the nature (acidic/basic/neutral) of each solution. In acidic media, blue litmus solution turns to red and in basic media, red litmus solution turns to blue.

Solution	**Effect on red litmus solution** (change in colour)	**Effect on blue litmus solution** (change in colour)	**Nature of solution found**
Sugar solution	No change	No change	neutral
Baking soda solution	Red changes to blue colour	No change	basic
Tamarind solution	No change	Blue changes to red colour	acidic
Salt solution (neutral)	No change	No change	neutral

Q. 24 You are provided with three test tubes *A*, *B* and *C* as shown in figure with different liquids. What will you observe when you put

(a) a piece of blue litmus paper in each test tube?
(b) a piece of red litmus paper in each test tube?
(c) a few drops of phenolphthalein solution to each test tube?

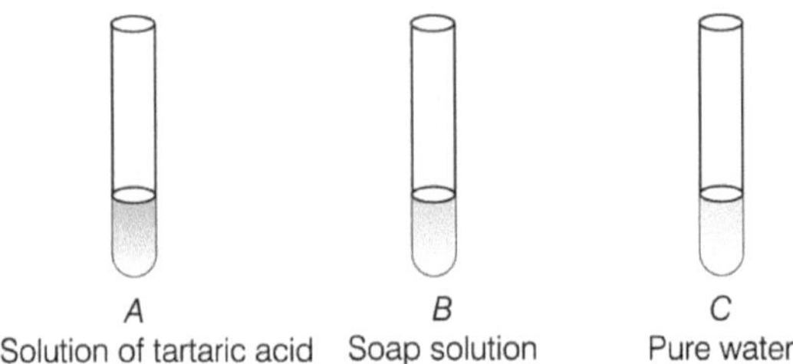

Ans.

Test tube	Effect on blue litmus paper	Effect on red litmus paper	Effect on phenolphthalein solution
A	Turns red	Remains red	Colourless
B	Remains blue	Turns blue	Pink colour
C	Remains blue	Remains red	Colourless

Q. 25 Paheli observed that most of the fish in the pond of her village were gradually dying. She also observed that the waste of a factory in their village is flowing into the pond which probably caused the fish to die.

(a) Explain why the fish were dying?
(b) If the factory waste is acidic in nature, how can it be neutralised?

Ans. (a) If the wastes of a factory flow into waterbodies, it can cause a threat to the lives of aquatic creatures and to anybody who drink the water. Since, the acids present in the factory waste will kill the fish and other aquatic organisms.

(b) If the factory waste is acidic in nature, it can be neutralised by adding basic substances.

Q. 26 Explain two neutralisation reactions related to daily life situations.

Ans. (a) **Ant bite** When an ant bite injects the acidic liquid (formic acid) into the skin, the effect of the acid can be neutralised by rubbing moist baking soda (sodium hydrogen carbonate) or calamine solution, which contains zinc carbonate.

(b) **Indigestion** Our stomach contains hydrochloric acid. It helps us to digest food but too much of acid in the stomach causes indigestion. Sometimes, indigestion is painful. To relieve indigestion, we take an antacid such as milk of magnesia which contains magnesium hydroxide. It neutralises the effect of excessive acid.

6

Physical and Chemical Changes

Multiple Choice Questions (MCQs)

Q. 1 Which one of the following is a physical change?

(a) Rusting of iron
(b) Combustion of magnesium ribbon
(c) Burning of candle
(d) Melting of wax

Ans. *(d)* Rusting, combustion and burning involve chemical changes.
Melting of wax is a physical change.

Q. 2 Which one of the following is a chemical change?

(a) Twinkling of stars
(b) Cooking of vegetables
(c) Cutting of fruits
(d) Boiling of water

Ans. *(b)* Cooking of vegetables involves many chemical changes.

Q. 3 A chemical change may involve

(a) change in colour only
(b) change in temperature only
(c) evolution of gas only
(d) All of the these

Ans. *(d)* Chemical reactions may accompany change in colour, evolution of heat and gas etc.

Q. 4 Which of the following are true when milk changes into curd?

(i) Its state is changed from liquid to semi-solid.
(ii) It changes colour.
(iii) It changes taste.
(iv) The change cannot be reversed.

Choose the correct option.

(a) (i) and (ii)
(b) (ii) and (iii)
(c) (i), (iii) and (iv)
(d) (i) to (iv)

Ans. *(c)* Colour of milk does not change after it convert into curds.

Q. 5 A man painted his main gate made up of iron, to

(i) prevent it from rusting
(ii) protect it from the sun
(iii) make it look beautiful
(iv) make it dust free

Which of the above statements is/are correct?

(a) (i) and (ii) (b) (ii) and (iii) (c) Only (ii) (d) (i) and (iii)

Ans. ***(d)*** Iron gate does not need to be protected from sun. Paints cannot avoid dust. To prevent rusting of iron gate, we do paint on it. Painting makes it beautiful.

Q. 6 Iron pillar near the Qutub Minar in Delhi is famous for the following facts. Which of these facts is responsible for its long stability?

(a) It is more than 7 m high
(b) It weighs about 6000 kg
(c) It was built more than 1600 yrs ago
(d) It has no rust after such long period

Ans. ***(d)*** Composition of the iron pillar make it resistant of rusting. It has not rusted after such a long period.

Q. 7 Galvanisation is a process used to prevent rusting of which of the following?

(a) Iron (b) Zinc (c) Aluminium (d) Copper

Ans. ***(a)*** Layer of zinc is applied on iron surface in galvanisation process to save it from rusting.

Q. 8 Paheli's mother made a concentrated sugar syrup by dissolving sugar in hot water. On cooling, crystals of sugar got separated.
This indicates a

(a) physical change that can be reversed
(b) chemical change that can be reversed
(c) physical change that cannot be reversed
(d) chemical change that cannot be reversed

Ans. ***(a)*** Crystallisation is a physical process and can be reversed.

Q. 9 Which of the following statements is incorrect for a chemical reaction?

(a) Heat may be given out but never absorbed
(b) Sound may be produced
(c) A colour change may take place
(d) A gas may be evolved

Ans. ***(a)*** Heat may be given out as well as absorbed during chemical reactions.

Q. 10 Two drops of dilute sulphuric acid were added to 1g of copper sulphate powder and then small amount of hot water was added to dissolve it (Step I). On cooling, beautiful blue coloured crystals got separated (Step II). Step I and Step II are

(a) physical and chemical changes respectively
(b) chemical and physical changes respectively
(c) both physical change
(d) both chemical change

Ans. ***(c)*** Step I and Step II are both physical change.

Very Short Answer Type Questions

Q. 11 State whether the following statements are true or false.

(a) When a candle burns, both physical and chemical changes take place.
(b) Anaerobic bacteria digest animal waste and produce biogas.
(c) Ships suffer a lot of damage though they are painted.
(d) Stretching of rubber band is not a physical change.

Ans. (a) True, the wax meting is a physical process, while combustion of wax is chemical process,
(b) True
(c) True, salty water of sea causes faster rusting of iron.
(d) False, stretching of rubber band is a physical change.

Q. 12 Melting of wax is a change where a solid changes to liquid state. Give one more such change which you observe in your surroundings.

Ans. Melting of ice is also a change where solid changes into liquid state.

Q. 13 What kind of change is shown by tearing of paper?

Ans. Tearing of paper is a physical change although, it cannot be reversed.

Short Answer Type Questions

Q. 14 Match the items of Column I with the items of Column II.

	Column I		Column II
(a)	Large crystals	(i)	Turn lime water milky
(b)	Depositing a layer of zinc on iron	(ii)	Physical change
(c)	Souring of milk	(iii)	Rust
(d)	Carbon dioxide	(iv)	Sugar candy (mishri)
(e)	Iron oxide	(v)	Chemical change
(f)	Dissolving common salt in water	(vi)	Galvanisation

Ans. The correct matching is as given:
(a)—(iv), (b)—(vi), (c)—(v), (d)—(i), (e)—(iii), (f)—(ii)

Note • *Carbon dioxide form calcium carbonate with lime water* [$Ca(OH)_2$] *and turns it milky. It is a chemical change.*
• *During rusting, iron reacts with moist oxygen to form iron oxide, which is called rust.*

Q. 15 Fill in the blanks.

(a) Making sugar solution is a .... change.
(b) A physical change is generally ....
(c) Grinding of wheat grain changes its size. It is a .... change.
(d) Iron benches kept in lawns and gardens get .... It is a .... change because a new .... is formed.

Ans. (a) physical (b) reversible
(c) physical (d) rusted, chemical, substance

Q. 16 Classify the following processes into physical or chemical changes.

(a) Beating of aluminium metal to make aluminium foil
(b) Digestion of food
(c) Cutting of a log of wood into pieces
(d) Burning of crackers

Ans. Physical changes are beating of aluminium metal to make aluminium foil and cutting of a log of wood into pieces. Chemical changes are digestion of food and burning of crackers.

Q. 17 Write word equations for two chemical reactions with the help of materials given in the box.

Air, copper sulphate, iron, vinegar, iron oxide, carbon dioxide, iron sulphate, copper, lime water, water

Ans. (i) Iron + air + water ⟶ iron oxide
(ii) Copper sulphate + iron ⟶ iron sulphate + copper

Q. 18 Explain the following:

(a) Lime water turns milky on passing carbon dioxide gas through it.
(b) Bubbles are produced when acetic acid is added to a solution of sodium hydrogen carbonate.

Ans. (a) When carbon dioxide (CO_2) reacts with lime water [$Ca(OH)_2$], then calcium carbonate ($CaCO_3$) and water (H_2O) is formed.

$$Ca(OH)_2 + CO_2 \longrightarrow CaCO_3 + H_2O$$

Calcium carbonate being insoluble white powder gives milky appearance to water.

(b) When baking soda ($NaHCO_3$) is added to acetic acid (CH_3COOH) then carbon dioxide (CO_2) gas is formed which causes appearance of bubbles.

$CH_3COOH + NaHCO_3 \longrightarrow CO_2 +$ other substance

Long Answer Type Questions

Q. 19 Give two examples for each of the following cases:

(a) Physical changes which are reversible.
(b) Physical changes which are not reversible.
(c) Chemical changes

Ans. (a) (i) Folding of paper (ii) Melting of ice
(b) (i) Tearing of paper (ii) Breaking of glass
(c) (i) Reaction between vinegar and baking soda
(ii) Burning of a matchstick

Q. 20 Give an example of a chemical reaction for each of the following situations:

(a) A change in colour is observed.
(b) A gas is evolved.
(c) Sound is produced.

Ans. (a) Chemical reaction between copper sulphate solution and iron metal. In this reaction, blue colour of copper sulphate solution changes to light green colour due to the formation of iron sulphate.

$$\underset{\text{(Blue)}}{\text{Copper sulphate}} + \underset{\text{(Grey)}}{\text{Iron}} \longrightarrow \underset{\text{(Light green)}}{\text{Iron sulphate}} + \underset{\text{(Brown)}}{\text{Copper}}$$

(b) When baking soda and vinegar are mixed together then a chemical change takes place and bubbles of carbon dioxide gas are formed along with some other substances.

$$\underset{\text{(Sodium hydrogen carbonate)}}{\text{Baking soda}} + \underset{\text{(Acetic acid)}}{\text{Vinegar}} \longrightarrow \text{Sodium acetate} + \text{Carbon dioxide} + \text{Water}$$

(c) Explosion of a firework produces heat, light, sound and unpleasant gases. Explosion of a firework is a chemical change.

Q. 21 **If you leave a piece of iron in the open for a few days, it acquires a film of brownish substance, called rust.**

(a) Do you think rust is different from iron?

(b) Can you change rust back into iron by some simple method?

(c) Do you think formation of rust on iron is a chemical change?

(d) Give two other examples of a similar type of change.

Ans. (a) Yes, rust is iron oxide (Fe_2O_3). Thus, rust and iron are not the same substance.

(b) No, rusting of iron is a chemical change because in this reaction, a new substance, rust (iron oxide) is formed. It cannot be reversed by any simple method.

(c) Yes, rusting of iron is a chemical change. During the rusting of iron, it combines with the oxygen in the presence of water (moisture) to form a new compound 'iron oxide'. This iron oxide is a rust.

$$\text{Iron} + \text{Oxygen} + \underset{\text{(From damp air)}}{\text{Water}} \longrightarrow \underset{\text{(Rust)}}{\text{Iron oxide}}$$

It is a permanent change which cannot be reversed back.

So, rusting of iron is a chemical change.

(d) Two other examples are:

(i) Setting of curd from milk.

(ii) Burning of magnesium ribbon to form magnesium oxide.

Q. 22 **A student took a solution of copper sulphate in a beaker and put a clean iron nail into it and left it for about an hour.**

(a) What changes do you expect?

(b) Are these changes chemical in nature?

(c) Write a word equation for the chemical change, if any.

Ans. (a) (i) Colour of the solution in the beaker changes from blue to green.

(ii) A brown coloured deposit is found on the surface of the iron nail.

(b) The changes are chemical in nature as new substances, iron sulphate (green) and copper (brown) are formed.

(c) $$\underset{\text{(Blue)}}{\text{Copper sulphate}} + \text{Iron} \longrightarrow \underset{\text{(Green)}}{\text{Iron sulphate}} + \underset{\text{(Brown)}}{\text{Copper}}$$

7

Weather, Climate and Adaptation of Animals to Climate

Multiple Choice Questions (MCQs)

Q. 1 The maximum and minimum temperature displayed daily in the weather bulletin refers to the

(a) highest day temperature and lowest night temperature of the day
(b) highest day temperature and highest night temperature of the month
(c) temperature recorded at 12 noon and at mid night (00.00 h)
(d) average highest temperature of day and average lowest temperature of night

Ans. *(a)* The highest temperature reached during the day is called the 'maximum' temperature and the 'lowest' temperature during the night is called the 'minimum' temperature.

These temperatures are recorded to prepare weather reports, by using a special thermometer, called **Maximum** and **minimum thermometer**.

Q. 2 Out of the given definitions, which is the most appropriate definition of climate?

(a) Changes in weather conditions in a year
(b) Average weather pattern of many years
(c) Change in weather pattern in a few years
(d) Weather conditions during summer

Ans. *(b)* The average weather pattern taken over a long time (say 25 years) is called the climate of that place. Temperature, rainfall, altitude and location with respect to the sea are factors which affect climate.

Q. 3 Which of the following briefly describes the desert climate?

(a) Hot and humid
(b) Dry and humid
(c) Hot and dry
(d) Hot and wet

Ans *(c)* In the desert, the temperature of climate is high during most part of the year and receives very little rainfall. This is called the hot and dry climate, e.g. Western region of India such as Rajasthan.

Q. 4 Paheli went to a wildlife sanctuary, where she saw dense vegetation of trees, shrubs, herbs and also a variety of animals like monkeys, birds, elephants, snakes, frogs, etc. The most likely location of this sanctuary is in the

(a) temperate region
(b) tropical region
(c) polar region
(d) coastal region

Ans. *(b)* Since Paheli saw a large variety of plants and animals, the likely location could be tropical region. The highly favourable climatic conditions (continuous warmth and rain) of these regions supports a wide variety of living organisms.

Q. 5 Given below are some adaptive features of animals.

(i) Layer of fat under the skin
(ii) Long, curved and sharp claws
(iii) Slippery body
(iv) Thick white fur

Which of them is/are the adaptive features of a polar bear?

(a) Only (i)
(b) (i) and (ii)
(c) (i), (ii) and (iii)
(d) (i), (ii) and (iv)

Ans. *(d)* Polar bear is a large white bear that lives in North polar regions of the Earth. For living in extremely cold climate, it has many adaptations, such as:

(i) Layer of fat under skin for insulation.
(ii) Long curved and sharp claws to walk and run on slippery ice.
(iii) Thick white fur. White colour protects it from predators and thick layer keep it warm.
(iv) Other features are rounded body, small ears and strong sense of smell.

Q. 6 Which of the following statements is incorrect for penguins?

(a) They huddle together
(b) They cannot swim
(c) They have webbed feet
(d) They have streamlined body

Ans. *(b)* Penguins have streamlined body, flipper-like wings and webbed feet which make them good swimmers. This helps in catching their prey (fish).

Q. 7 Read the following environmental conditions of tropical rainforests.

(i) Hot and humid climate
(ii) Unequal lengths of day and night
(iii) Abundant rainfall
(iv) Abundant light and moisture

Identify the conditions from the above list that are responsible for the presence of large number of plants and animals in tropical rainforests.

(a) (i) and (ii)
(b) (i) and (iii)
(c) (i), (iii) and (iv)
(d) (ii) and (iv)

Ans. *(c)* The environmental conditions in tropical rainforests are highly suitable for supporting an enormous number and a variety of plants and animals. The conditions are:

(i) Hot and humid climate because of its location around equator.

(ii) Abundant rainfall, light and moisture.

Q. 8 The coldest region on the earth is the

(a) polar region
(b) tropical region
(c) temperate region
(d) coastal region

Ans. *(a)* The polar regions of the earth have an extreme cold climate. These regions are covered with snow and are very cold for most part of the year.
The options, i.e. **tropical region**, has a hot climate, **temperate regions** do not have extremes of temperature and precipitation and **coastal region** has mild climate, with hot summers and cool winters.

Q. 9 Choose the odd one from the following options.

(a) Thick layer of fat under the skin
(b) White fur
(c) Long grasping tail
(d) Wide and large feet with sharp claws

Ans. *(c)* Long grasping tail is the odd one. The other options describe the adaptations of polar bear. They have short and compact tail, that helps them to conserve heat.

Very Short Answer Type Questions

Q. 10 A fish dies when taken out of water, whereas a wall lizard will die if kept under water. Mention the term used to describe such abilities that allow fish and lizard to survive in their respective habitats.

Ans. 'Adaptation' is the term used to describe such abilities that allows an organism to survive in their respective habitats, e.g. fishes have gills that allow them to live in water. While a wall lizard has lungs to perform the same function (i.e. respiration) on land.

Hence, adaptations are specific body features (habits) which enable an organism to live in a particular habitat.

Q. 11 Give one example of an animal that can live both in water and on land.

Ans. Amphibians are the animals that can live in both water and on land, e.g. frog, that has lungs for breathing on land and uses it's skin under water for the same purpose.

Q. 12 State whether the following statements are True or False. Correct the false statements.

(a) It is easy to predict weather rather than climate.

(b) Since very few prey are available, polar bear does not need to have strong sense of smell.

(c) Penguins stick together to fight the cold polar climate.

(d) Tropical rainforests are cool and humid throughout the year because of heavy rains all the time.

Ans. (a) False, It is easy to predict **climate** rather than **weather**.

(b) False, Since very few prey are available, polar bear **needs** to have strong sense of smell.

(c) True.

(d) False, Tropical rainforests are **hot** and humid throughout the year because of heavy rains all the time.

Q. 13 Unscramble the following words using the hints given against them.

(a) MATLICE (Hint : weather pattern in a region over a period of time)

(b) AROPL (Hint : coolest region on earth)

(c) THEHMEOMRET (Hint : used to measure temperature)

(d) UHIDYTMI (Hint : feature of weather)

Ans. The correct words are as follows:

(a) CLIMATE (b) POLAR (c) THERMOMETER (d) HUMIDITY

Short Answer Type Questions

Q. 14 Match the animals mentioned in Column I with their characteristic features given in Column II.

	Column I		Column II
(a)	Red- eyed frog	(i)	Very sensitive hearing
(b)	Penguin	(ii)	Streamlined body
(c)	Tiger	(iii)	Silver-white mane
(d)	Lion-tailed macaque	(iv)	Sticky pads on feet

Ans. The correct matching is as given

(a)—(iv), (b)—(ii), (c)—(i), (d)–(iii)

(a) Red-eyed tree frogs have sticky pads on their feet that allow them to stay balanced and in place.

(b) Penguins have streamlined body that help them in swimming.

(c) Tiger has very sensitive acute hearing so that it can detect potential prey in the bushes and grasses around them.

(d) The lion-tailed macaque has an outstanding characteristic that is its silver-white mane which surrounds the head from the cheeks down to its chin. It frames the face-like lion.

Q. 15 Why is it difficult to predict the weather of a place, while it is easy to predict its climate?

Ans. Weather is the day-to-day condition of the atmosphere at a place with respect to the temperature, humidity, rainfall, etc. It is a complex phenomenon which can vary over a short period of time and thus, it is difficult to predict the weather of a place.

On the contrary, it is easier to predict climate as it is the average weather pattern taken for a long time.

Q. 16 Name two animals each that live in polar regions and tropical rainforests.

Ans. **Polar regions** Polar bear/penguin/ reindeer/musk/oxen.

Tropical rainforests Red-eyed frog /elephants/lion-tailed macaque/ lion and tiger. [any two]

Q. 17 Write two common adaptive features of a polar bear which help in keeping it warm.

Ans. Adaptive features of a polar bear that help in keeping it warm are as follows:

(i) **Two thick layers of white fur on its body** Prevents the loss of heat.

(ii) **Thick layer of fat under its skin** Insulates it against heat loss.

Q. 18 Mention two adaptive features of penguin that help it in swimming.

Ans. Adaptive features of penguin that help it in swimming are as follows:

(i) **Streamlined body,** reduces drag in water.

(ii) **Webbed feet** and flipper-like wings.

Q. 19 Differentiate between

(a) Weather and climate
(b) Humidity and rainfall
(c) Climates of polar region and tropical rainforest
(d) Maximum and minimum temperatures of the day

Ans. (a) **Weather** is the daily fluctuation in temperature, humidity, etc. While **climate** is the average weather pattern of a place.

(b) **Humidity** indicates the wetness of a place due to the presence of moisture in the atmosphere, while **rainfall** is the drops of water that falls from clouds on the ground.

(c) **Polar region** remains very cold for most part of the year, whereas **tropical rainforest** is hot and humid.

(d) **Maximum** and **minimum temperatures** of the day indicate highest and lowest recorded temperatures, respectively.

Long Answer Type Questions

Q. 20 Fill in the blanks in the paragraph given below.

Weather of a place is the day to day condition of the ...(a)... with respect to ...(b)... , ...(c)..., ...(d)..., ...(e)... , at that place, while climate is the ...(f)... weather pattern taken over many years.

Ans. (a) atmosphere (b) temperature

(c) humidity (d) rainfall

(e) wind speed (f) average

Q. 21 Given below is a list of climatic conditions and some examples of animals. Read them carefully and place the items in the relevant columns as shown:

Penguin, Gorilla, Monkey, Reindeer, Assam, Greenland, Sun does not rise for six months, Hot and humid climate. Days and nights are almost equal in length throughout the year, Winter temperature around –37°C, Western Ghats

Tropical rainforest	Polar region
Hot and humid climate	Penguin

Ans. The terms in the relevant column can be placed as shown below :

Tropical rainforest	Polar region
Hot and humid climate	Penguin
Gorilla	Reindeer
Monkey	Greenland
Assam	Sun does not rise for six months
Days and nights are almost equal in length throughout the year	
Western Ghats	Winter temperature around – 37°C

8

Wind, Storm and Cyclone

Multiple Choice Questions (MCQs)

Q. 1 A fire alarm usually detects smoke in case of fire. Where should such an alarm be placed in a room?

(a) Near the door (b) On the floor (c) On any wall (d) On the ceiling

Ans. *(d)* In case of fire, the air above the fire becomes hotter and rises up. So, the alarm should be placed on the ceiling in a room, it can detect the smoke rising up.

Q. 2 Four schematic diagrams are shown below to depict the direction of sea breeze. Which of them gives the correct direction?

(a)

(b)

(c)

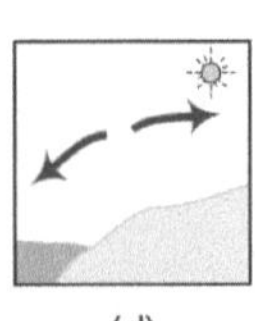
(d)

Ans. *(c)* In summer, during the day the land becomes warm and the air over the land gets heated and rises. This causes the cooler air blow from the sea towards the land.

The warm air from the land moves towards the sea to complete the cycle. The air from the sea, moving towards the land is called sea breeze.

Q. 3 Figure shows a child blowing air with a straw near the opening of another straw which has its other end in a soft drink bottle. It was observed that the level of the soft drink in the straw rises up as soon as air is blown over its open end. Which one of the following best explains the reason for rise in level of the drink?

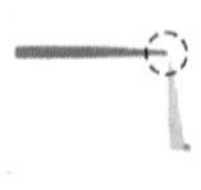

(a) Blowing of air decreases pressure over the opening of the straw
(b) The straw of the soft drink bottle collapses when air is blown over its open end
(c) Blowing of air warms up the air inside the straw
(d) Blowing of air increases the pressure on the surface of soft drink in the bottle

Ans. *(a)* Blowing of air decreases the pressure over the opening of the straw due to which the level of the soft drink in the straw rises up.

Q. 4 Following are precautions, one must take in case a storm is accompanied by lightning.

(i) Do not take shelter under tree.
(ii) Do not take shelter under an umbrella with a metallic end.
(iii) Do not take shelter in open garages, storage sheds, etc.
(iv) Do not take shelter in a bus in the open.

Which one of these is not correct?

(a) (i) (b) (ii) (c) (iii) (d) (iv)

Ans. *(d)* Because a car or a bus is a safe place to take shelter in such a situation.

Q. 5 Which of the following place is most likely to be affected by a cyclone?

(a) Mumbai (b) Puri
(c) Goa (d) Porbandar

Ans. *(b)* Puri is most likely to be affected by a cyclone because this city lies near the coastal area.

Q. 6 A curtain is hanging at the entrance of a room. A long corridor runs at right angles to the door, that is parallel to the curtain. If a strong wind blows along the corridor, the curtain will

(a) get pushed inside the room
(b) get pushed outside the room
(c) get collected towards one end/ swirled
(d) remain unaffected

Ans. *(b)* If a strong wind blows along the corridor, then the air pressure there increases and the curtain gets pushed outside the room.

Very Short Answer Type Questions

Q. 7 Why is Chandigarh unlikely to be affected by a cyclone?

Ans. Chandigarh is unlikely to be affected by a cyclone because it is not near the sea or ocean.

Q. 8 Name the ocean which is mainly responsible to bring rain bearing monsoon winds to Kerala coast in June every year.

Ans. An Indian ocean is mainly responsible to bring rain bearing monsoon winds to Kerala coast in June every year.

Q. 9 Fill in the blanks.

(a) Air around us exerts ....

(b) The moving air is called ....

(c) The main cause of wind movement is uneven ....

(d) High speed wind can cause cyclone in regions of .... pressure.

Ans. (a) Pressure, it is because of this pressure that the leaves of trees or banners flutter when the air moves.

(b) Wind

(c) Heating, wind currents are generated due to the uneven heating on the earth (i.e. between the equator and the poles and of land and water).

(d) Low, a very low–pressure system, with very high speed winds revolving around it, forms a cyclone.

Q. 10 State whether the following statements are True or False.

(a) If wind flows from land to the ocean, then it is day time.

(b) A very high pressure system with very high speed wind surrounding it forms a cyclone.

(c) The coast line of India is not vulnerable to cyclones.

(d) Warm air is lighter than cool air.

Ans. (a) False, if wind blow from land to the ocean, then it is night time because at night, the water cools down more slowly than the land. So, the cool wind from the land moves towards the ocean.

(b) False, a very low pressure system, with very high speed winds revolving around it, forms a cyclone.

(c) False, the whole coast line of India is vulnerable to cyclones, particularly the east coast.

(d) True, on heating the air expands and occupies more space. When the same thing occupies more space, then it becomes lighter.

Q. 11 To expel hot air out of the kitchen, *A* has an exhaust fan fitted on the window of her kitchen and *B* has a similar exhaust fan fitted on the wall near the ceiling of her kitchen. Which of the exhaust fan will expel the hot air more effectively? Explain why.

Ans. *B*'s exhaust fan will expel the hot air more effectively because hot air rises up and her fan is at greater height than *A*'s.

Q. 12 Why is it advisable not to shut all the doors and windows during a storm?

Ans. During storms, heavy winds passing over the house creates a low pressure. The high pressure inside the house tries to fill the low pressure outside. Since, this pressure is stuck inside the house, therefore, it pushes or lifts the roof off.

So, unless the house is well ventilated, the roof is more likely to blow off in a strong wind.

Q. 13 A flat in Mumbai with a balcony facing the sea has some clothes hung on a clothes line in the balcony. Towards which direction, the clothes will be blown in the afternoon? Explain it.

Ans. In the afternoon, the land gets heated faster than the water. The air over the land becomes hotter and rises up, creating a drop in pressure. This causes the winds to flow from the sea towards the land.

Thus, the clothes will be blown towards the house because of sea breeze flowing towards the land.

Q. 14 **Figure shows a diagrammatic representation of trees in the afternoon along a sea coast. State on which side is the sea, *A* or *B*? Give reasons for your choice.**

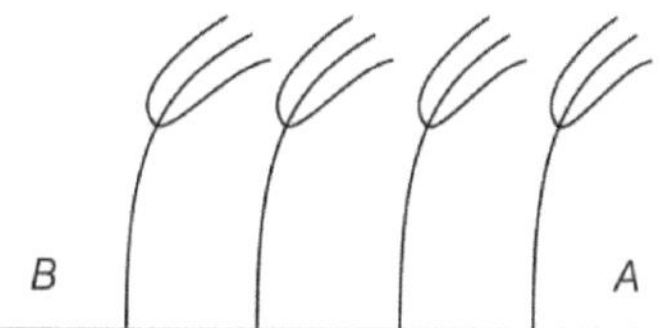

Ans. In the afternoon, the air over the land becomes hotter and rises up creating a drop in pressure there. Thus, the wind blows from sea to land, so the sea is on *B* side.

Q. 15 **A flag mounted on a flag post near the sea coast flutters in the direction of sea. At what time of the day does this happen — at mid-night or in the afternoon?**

Ans. At night, the water cools down more slowly than the land. So, at mid-night, cool wind from the land moves towards the sea. Therefore, at mid-night the flag mounted on a flag post near the sea coast flutters in the direction of sea.

Short Answer Type Questions

Q. 16 **Match the Column I with Column II. There can be more than one match.**

	Column I		Column II
(a)	On heating air	(i)	descends
(b)	On cooling air	(ii)	expands
		(iii)	contracts
		(iv)	rises

Ans. The correct matching is as given:

(a)–(ii) and (iv), **(b)**–(i) and (iii).

Air expands on heating and contracts on cooling. Warm air rises up, whereas comparatively cooler air descends (moves down) to that place.

Q. 17 **Paheli kept an empty bottle made of plastic inside a refrigerator. After few hours, when she opened the refrigerator, she found the bottle had collapsed. Explain the possible reason.**

Ans. On cooling the air, contraction of air takes place. So, the air inside the bottle contracts due to the low temperature. Hence, the bottle collapses due to the outside pressure.

Q. 18 When strong/high speed wind blows, an umbrella held upright at times gets upturned. Explain the reason.

Ans. High speed wind passing over the umbrella creates low pressure above the umbrella. Therefore, the pressure below the umbrella upturns it.

Q. 19 Suggest some precautions to be taken to prevent the roof of a tin sheet from flying away during a fierce wind storm.

Ans. Some precautions are:

(i) Put heavy stones on it. (ii) Screw it tight.

Long Answer Type Questions

Q. 20 Describe an activity to demonstrate that warm air is lighter than cool air.

Ans. (i) Take two paper bags of the same size.

(ii) Hang the two bags in the inverted position on the two ends of a wooden stick.

(iii) Tie a piece of thread in the middle of stick and hold the stick by the thread in balance, as shown in the figure (*A*).

(iv) Place a burning candle below one of the bags as shown in figure (*B*).

(v) You will observe that the balance of the bags is disturbed.

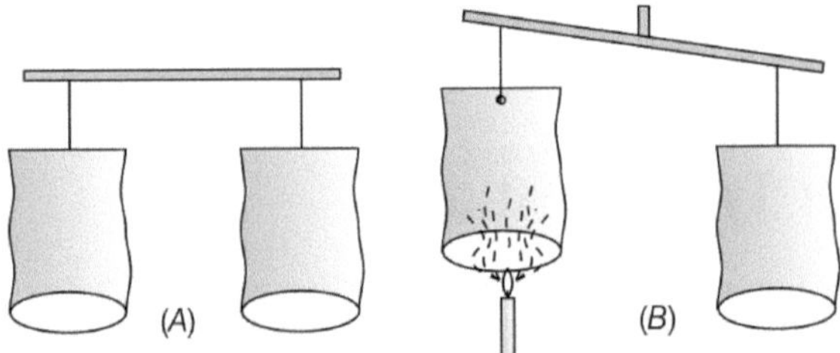

This activity indicates that as the warm air rises up it pushes the bag above the candle. This is because on heating, air expands and occupies more space. When same thing occupies more space, it becomes lighter. Thus, we can conclude that warm air is lighter than cool air.

Q. 21 The picture shows tree line along the sea coast on an island near the equator. As shown, the tree tops are permanently bent in one direction. Are the trees bend towards the sea or away from it? Explain.

Ans. In the given figure, the tree line along the sea coast on an island near the equator shows that tree tops are permanently bent in one direction, i.e. towards the land. The reason behind this movement of trees is that during the day time, the wind blows from sea to land because at this time, land gets warmer more quickly than sea.

This makes the air of land, warm and lighter which is raised up in the sky. Therefore, the top of the bent trees shows the moving direction of wind from sea to land.

Q. 22 Identify the names of six natural phenomena from the following word diagram given as figure.

G	C	H	T	H	T	E	N	M	R
R	C	Y	H	O	O	N	C	Z	P
V	L	O	U	E	R	O	E	R	T
A	N	C	N	A	N	N	L	C	L
H	T	H	D	B	A	D	A	P	I
L	U	N	E	K	D	C	Y	D	G
H	U	R	R	I	C	A	N	E	H
W	C	T	S	L	M	N	O	P	T
M	Y	O	T	Y	P	H	O	O	N
O	C	R	O	H	C	T	P	Q	I
C	L	N	R	U	A	Y	R	S	N
F	O	A	M	R	N	P	T	U	G
P	N	D	X	R	E	H	Y	E	N
Z	E	O	A	I	O	U	N	Y	B

Ans.

G	C	H	T	H	T	E	N	M	R
R	C	Y	H	O	O	N	C	Z	P
V	L	O	U	E	R	O	E	R	T
A	N	C	N	A	N	N	L	C	L
H	T	H	D	B	A	D	A	P	I
L	U	N	E	K	D	C	Y	D	G
H	U	R	R	I	C	A	N	E	H
W	C	T	S	L	M	N	O	P	T
M	Y	O	T	Y	P	H	O	O	N
O	C	R	O	H	C	T	P	Q	I
C	L	N	R	U	A	Y	R	S	N
F	O	A	M	R	N	P	T	U	G
P	N	D	X	R	E	H	Y	E	N
Z	E	O	A	I	O	U	N	Y	B

The natural phenomena in the given above crossword are cyclone, thunder, storm and lightning, typhoon and hurricane. A cyclone is called 'hurricane in the American continent and 'typhoon' in Philippines and Japan.

9

Soil

Multiple Choice Questions (MCQs)

Q. 1 The microorganisms present in the soil require moisture (water) and nutrients for growth and survival. Choose from the options below, the habitat (place) where the soil has plenty of water and nutrients.

(a) Desert (b) Forest (c) Open field (d) Cricket ground

Ans. *(b)* The microorganism present in the soil having plenty of water and nutrients are present in the habitat of forest.

Q. 2 Availability of water and minerals in the soil for maximum absorption by roots is in the

(a) B-horizon (b) C-horizon (c) A-horizon (d) Surface of soil

Ans. *(c)* Availability of water and minerals in the soil for maximum absorption by roots is in A-horizon. A-horizon is called the topsoil and this layer is generally soft, porous and can retain more water.

Q. 3 Soil conservation measures are mainly aimed at protecting which of the following?

(a) Plants (b) Topsoil (c) Subsoil (d) Soil organisms

Ans. *(b)* Soil conservation measures mainly aim at protecting topsoil, which is rich in humus and nutrients making it fertile to grow plants.

Q. 4 Read the following statements with reference to soil.

(i) Weathering is a very fast process of soil formation.
(ii) Percolation of water is faster in sandy soils.
(iii) Loamy soil contains only sand and clay.
(iv) Topsoil contains the maximum amount of humus.

Choose the correct statements from the above.

(a) (ii) and (iv) (b) (i) and (iii) (c) (ii) and (iii) (d) (i) and (ii)

Ans. *(a)* Statements (ii) and (iv) are correct with reference to soil while (i) weathering is a slow process of soil formation and (iii) loamy soil consists of sand, clay and silt along with humus.

Very Short Answer Type Questions

Q. 5 Soil has particles of different sizes. Arrange the words given below in increasing order of their particle size.
Rock, clay, sand, gravel, silt

Ans. The soil particles with the increasing order of their particle sizes can be shown as:
Clay < Silt < Sand < Gravel < Rock

Q. 6 The components of loamy soil are ...., ... and ....

Ans. Sand, Silt and Clay

Q. 7 Read the following statements and give the appropriate terms for each of them.

(a) The process of breakdown of rocks by the action of wind, water, sunlight.
(b) Removal of topsoil during heavy rains or strong winds.
(c) Accumulation of wastes in the soil generated by human activity which alter the features of soil.
(d) The process of movement of water into deeper layers of soil.

Ans. The terms for the above described statements are as follows:
(a) Weathering (b) Soil erosion (c) Soil pollution (d) Percolation

Q. 8 Unscramble the following jumbled words related to soil.

(a) S U H U M
(b) I L O S F I P R O L E
(c) Z O I N O R H
(d) M O A L
(e) G I N R H E T W E A
(f) A T O N I E R P C L O

Ans. (a) HUMUS (b) SOIL PROFILE (c) HORIZON
(d) LOAM (e) WEATHERING (f) PERCOLATION

Short Answer Type Questions

Q. 9 Which of the following situations—'A' or 'B'—is advantageous for absorption of water and minerals? Why?
Situation 'A' : Growth and branching of roots in the C-horizon.
Situation 'B' : Growth and branching of roots in A and B-horizons.

Ans. Situation 'B' is advantageous for absorption of water and minerals. This is because A-horizon is top layer of soil and is rich in minerals and humus. The plant roots grow in the topsoil. The roots of some of the trees are however, able to reach B-horizon (subsoil). Subsoil is also rich in soluble minerals.

Q. 10 How can a farmer convert acidic soil into neutral soil?

Ans. The farmer can convert acidic soil into neutral soil by adding a small quantity of quicklime or slaked lime solution to the soil. Quick lime and slaked lime are bases and hence, react with the excess acid present in the soil and reduce its acidity.

Q. 11 Is it a good practice to remove grass and small plants that are growing in an open, unused field? Give reason to support your answer.

Ans. No, it is not a good practice to remove grass and small plants growing in an open, unused field because the plants cover the soil surface. Their roots bind the soil particles, holding and adhering them in place.

It helps in preventing the topsoil from being washed off during heavy rain, floods and winds. In this way, soil erosion is prevented and topsoil layer is preserved for growing more plants.

Q. 12 A man digging a pit found that he could dig with ease initially but digging became difficult as he went deeper. He could not dig beyond a depth 5 feet. Provide a suitable scientific explanations.

Ans. The man digging a pit could dig with ease initially because of the presence of topsoil and subsoil (mainly comprising of humus and nutrients). But as he digs deeper, he finds it difficult to dig beyond a depth of 5 feet as lower layers are made up of small partially weathered rocks with cracks, crevices and with bedrock which make it hard to dig.

Q. 13 Locate the following zones given as boxed items in figure which shows a diagram of soil profile.

Topsoil, subsoil, C-horizon, bedrock

Ans.

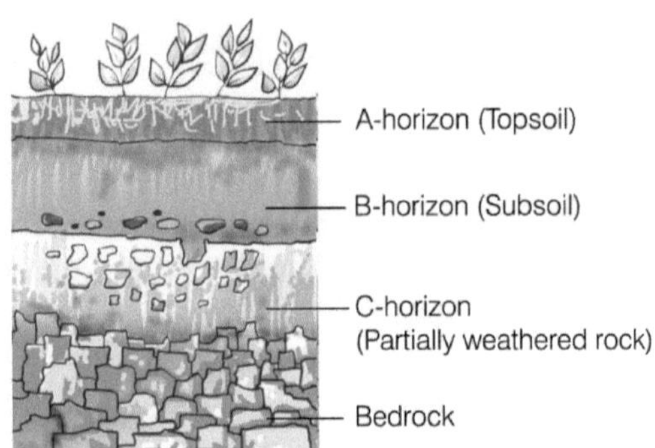

Q. 14 Rajasthan is a desert state in India. Once while travelling to Rajasthan by train, Boojho observed several streams and rivulets of rainwater during the journey but to his surprise, he did not see streams of water in the desert region even during rains. Help Boojho to find a suitable explanation for this.

Ans. Deserts are made up of sand, thus when the rainwater falls on land, it percolates immediately downwards in the spaces between sand particles. So, the streams of water in desert region are not visible even during rainy season.

Q. 15 Match the Column I with Column II.

	Column I		Column II
(a)	Earthworm	(i)	Sand and beaches.
(b)	Garden lizard	(ii)	Burrows in soil.
(c)	Crab	(iii)	Deep, narrow holes in dry soils.
(d)	Rodents	(iv)	Surface of soil.
(e)	Scorpion	(v)	Surface of shaded moist soils.
(f)	Snails and slugs	(vi)	A-horizon of moist soils.

Ans. The correct matching is as given

(a)—(vi), (b)—(iv), (c)—(i), (d)—(ii), (e)—(iii), (f)—(v)

Long Answer Type Questions

Q. 16 Continuously water-logged soils are disadvantageous for plant growth. Why?

Ans. Roots although underground possesses living cells that require oxygen for respiration and production of energy. They absorb oxygen that is present in the spaces between soil particles.

But in water-logged soils, water occupies spaces between soil particles and pushes the oxygen out into the atmosphere. Thus, roots are deprived of oxygen and this affects the plant growth.

Q. 17 Why is soil erosion relatively less in dense forests as compared to barren, open fields?

Ans. In dense forests, the tree cover (canopy) prevents rainwater from directly falling on the ground/soil. Also, the roots of vegetation bind the soil particles and hold them together. As a result, soil erosion is minimised.

But in barren open fields, the soil is exposed to the falling rain. The soil particles become loose due to the impact of raindrops and the flow of water carries them away. The flowing water further erodes the soil surface aggravating erosion.

Q. 18 Gardeners gently dig up the soil around the roots of garden herbs (plants) frequently. Give reasons.

Ans. (i) it enables easy root growth. (ii) for easier percolation of water.
(iii) for aerating the soil enabling air to get into deeper layers of soil.
(iv) for removing the weeds.

Q. 19 In towns and cities generally, the borewells have to be dug very deep to get water as compared to borewells dug in villages. Give suitable reasons.

Ans. The borewells have to be dug very deep in towns and cities to get water as compared to those in villages because

(i) excessive use of water in towns, depletes the groundwater.

(ii) towns and cities have asphalted roads and vast areas of soil are concreted. As a result, rainwater cannot percolate to recharge groundwater and the groundwater level further decreases.

Villages have larger areas of open soil surface and fewer asphalted roads and concrete surfaces. Thus, larger soil surface area is available for rainwater to percolate into the soil easily and recharge the groundwater. As a result, even shallow borewells yield water.

Q. 20 Several terms related to soil are hidden in the squares given as figure, spot them and make a list. Two examples are given for you.

G	R	P	E	L	I	F	O	R	P
W	H	U	M	U	S	S	G	M	E
E	A	B	S	R	G	A	I	G	R
A	E	T	C	G	V	N	K	N	C
T	R	H	E	G	E	D	Z	C	O
H	O	E	D	R	O	C	K	S	L
E	S	P	A	A	A	K	P	C	A
R	I	L	D	V	R	S	I	L	T
I	O	A	K	E	G	Q	M	A	I
N	N	N	T	L	S	G	H	Y	O
G	K	T	H	O	R	I	Z	O	N

Ans.

G	R	P	E	L	I	F	O	R	P
W	H	U	M	U	S	S	G	M	E
E	A	B	S	R	G	A	I	G	R
A	E	T	C	G	V	N	K	N	C
T	R	H	E	G	E	D	Z	C	O
H	O	E	D	R	O	C	K	S	L
E	S	P	A	A	A	K	P	C	A
R	I	L	D	V	R	S	I	L	T
I	O	A	K	E	G	Q	M	A	I
N	N	N	T	L	S	G	H	Y	O
G	K	T	H	O	R	I	Z	O	N

Humus, sand, water, clay, gravel, weathering, horizon, percolation, mineral, plant, erosion, profile, silt.

10

Respiration in Organisms

Multiple Choice Questions (MCQs)

Q. 1 Sometimes when we do heavy exercise, anaerobic respiration takes place in our muscle cells. What is produced during this process?

(a) Alcohol and lactic acid
(b) Alcohol and CO_2
(c) Lactic acid and CO_2
(d) Lactic acid only

Ans. *(d)* During heavy exercise, anaerobic respiration takes place in our muscle cells. This happens as the oxygen gets used up faster in our muscle cells than can be supplied by the blood.

To produce extra energy for exercise, the muscle cells shift to anaerobic respiration.

$$\text{Glucose} \xrightarrow[\text{in muscles, anaerobic respiration}]{\text{No oxygen}} \text{Lactic acid + Energy}$$

Q. 2 Yeast is used in wine and beer industries because it respires

(a) aerobically producing oxygen
(b) aerobically producing alcohol
(c) anaerobically producing alcohol
(d) anaerobically producing CO_2

Ans. *(c)* Yeast is a single-celled organism that respires anaerobically producing alcohol and carbon dioxide.

$$\text{Glucose} \xrightarrow[\text{Anaerobic respiration in yeast}]{\text{No oxygen}} \text{Alcohol} + CO_2 + \text{Energy}$$

The alcohol is used in wine and beer industry, while the CO_2 is used in bread making.

Q. 3 During the process of exhalation, the ribs move

(a) down and inwards
(b) up and inwards
(c) down and outwards
(d) up and outwards

Ans. *(a)* During exhalation, ribs move down and inwards, while diaphragm move upwards and relaxes. This reduces the size of the chest cavity and air is pushed out of the lungs.

Q. 4 Breathing is a process that

(i) provides O_2 to the body
(ii) breaks down food to release energy
(iii) helps the body to get rid of CO_2
(iv) produces water in the cells

Which of the following gives the correct combination of functions of breathing?

(a) (i) and (ii) (b) (ii) and (iii)
(c) (i) and (iii) (d) (ii) and (iv)

Ans. *(c)* Breathing is a process by which air rich in oxygen is taken inside the body and air rich in carbon dioxide is expelled from the body, with the help of respiratory organs.

It is a continuous process which goes on all the time and throughout the life of an organism.

Q. 5 Fish breathe with the help of gills which are richly supplied with blood vessels. The gills help the fish to

(a) take in oxygen from air
(b) take in oxygen dissolved in water
(c) absorb nutrients present in water
(d) release waste substances in water

Ans. *(b)* Fish has special organs called gills that help it to use oxygen dissolved in water. Gills are projections of the skin that are well supplied with blood vessels for exchange of gases.

Q. 6 Earthworms and frogs breathe through their skin because of which the skin of both the organisms is

(a) moist and rough (b) dry and rough
(c) dry and slimy (d) moist and slimy

Ans *(d)* Earthworms and frogs have moist and slimy skin that helps them to absorb the oxygen for respiration.

Q. 7 Mark the following statements as True or False. Correct the false statements.

(a) Oxygen breaks down glucose outside the cells of organisms.
(b) Frogs can breathe through their skin as well as lungs.
(c) Insects have spiracles on the lower surface of the body.
(d) Exhaled air has more percentage of CO_2 than inhaled air.

Ans. (a) False, Oxygen breaks down glucose inside the cells of organisms.
(b) True
(c) False, Insects have spiracles on the sides of the body.
(d) True

Q. 8 Fill in the blanks with suitable words.

(a) The roots of a plant take up oxygen from the .... trapped between the .... particles.
(b) Diaphragm forms the .... of the chest cavity.
(c) Exchange of gases in the leaves takes place with the help of ....
(d) Cockroaches breathe with the help of air tubes called ....

Ans. (a) air; soil (b) floor
(c) stomata (d) tracheae

Short Answer Type Questions

Q. 9 Pick the odd one out from each of the groups given below on the basis of respiratory organs. Give reason for your answer.

(a) Cockroach, grasshopper, snail, ant (b) Lizard, cow, earthworm, snake
(c) Crocodile, whale, dolphin, fish (d) Snake, tadpole, crow, goat

Ans. (a) Snail is the odd one, as it does not breathe by means of tracheae.

(b) Earthworm is the odd one, because it breathes through its skin and it does not have lungs.

(c) Fish is the odd one, as most fish breathe through their gills and do not have lungs.

(d) Tadpole is the odd one, as it breathes through gills and do not have lungs.

Q. 10 Which gas present in air is essential for aerobic respiration? What is the role of this gas during respiration?

Ans. Oxygen gas present in air is essential for aerobic respiration. It breaks down food and releases energy during respiration.

$$\text{Glucose} \xrightarrow{\text{Oxygen}} CO_2 + H_2O + \text{Energy}$$

Q. 11 On an average, an adult human being at rest breathes 15-18 times per minute. The breathing rate however, may differ under different conditions. Arrange the following activities given in the box in order of increasing breathing rates and give reason for your answer.
Sleeping, cycling, brisk walk, watching TV.

Ans. In order of increasing breathing rates, the activities are:

Sleeping < Watching TV < Brisk walk < Cycling

This is because whenever, a person does an activity, the breathing rate increases depending on the nature of the activity. With strenuous work to provide more oxygen to cells for more energy, the breathing rate further increases.

Therefore, sleeping has minimum breathing rate, while cycling (a physical exercise) has maximum rate.

Q. 12 On a very cold morning, Boojho and Paheli were talking with each other as they walked down to their school. They observed that the air coming out of their mouth looked like smoke. They were amused and wondered how it happened. Help them find the answer.

Ans. On a cold day, the warm and moist air exhaled by us condenses into mist, when it comes in contact with the cold air of the atmosphere. This looks like white smoke.

Q. 13 Whenever we feel drowsy or sleepy, we start yawning. Does yawning help us in anyway?

Ans. Yawning is the action of opening one's mouth wide while taking a long and deep breath of air. It is caused by insufficient oxygen in the body.

It usually occurs when we are drowsy or sleepy because our breathing rate slows down during these situation. The lungs do not get enough oxygen from the air for respiration.

Yawning helps in bringing more oxygen into the body through the wide open mouth.

Q. 14 Insects and leaves of a plant have pores through which they exchange gases with the atmosphere. Can you write two points of differences between these pores with respect to their position, number and extension into the body?

Ans. Pores present on the sides of insects are called **spiracles**, while pores present on the surface of leaves are called **stomata**. These structures are responsible for the exchange of gases with the atmosphere.

Differences between these two are as follows:

(i) Spiracles are fewer in number as compared to stomata.

(ii) Spiracles lead to an extensive network of tracheal system, which is absent in the leaves.

(iii) Spiracles are present on the sides of insect's body while stomata are present on the surface of leaves.

Long Answer Type Questions

Q. 15 Paheli participated in a 400 m race competition held at her school and won the race. When she came home she had mixed feelings of joy and pain as she had cramps in her leg muscles. After a massage, she was relieved of the pain. Answer the following questions related to situation.

(a) What can be the possible reasons for the pain in her legs?

(b) Why did she fell comfortable after a massage?

Ans. (a) Paheli had cramps in her leg muscles after running. She felt pain in her legs because of accumulation of lactic acid in the leg muscles. Lactic acid is formed due to the anaerobic respiration in the muscle cells after heavy exercise or running.

During heavy exercise, we require large amount of energy that is provided by muscle cells through anaerobic respiration (Oxygen present is used up for energy, so there is lack of oxygen).

Due to the partial breakup of glucose lactic acid is formed. It gets accumulated in the muscle cells and causes pain and muscle cramps.

(b) The massage or hot water bath gives relief from muscle cramps or pain, because it improves the circulation of blood leading to increased supply of oxygen to the muscle cells. It helps in complete breakdown of lactic acid into carbon dioxide and water.

Q. 16 Observe the given figures carefully and answer the following questions.

(a) The amount of CO_2 be the highest in which jar. Why?

(b) The amount of CO_2 be the lowest in which one and why?

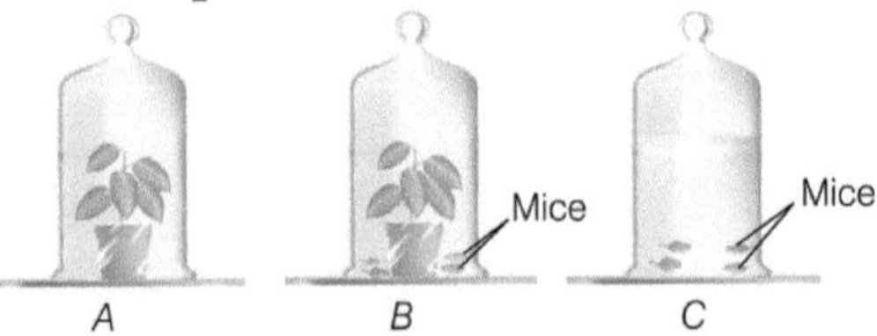

Ans. (a) The amount of CO_2 will be the highest in jar *C*. It is because the mice kept under the jar will breathe out CO_2 continuously increasing its amount in the jar.

In other jars, the CO_2 present inside will be used up by the plants for photosynthesis. So, its amount will decrease.

(b) The amount of CO_2 will be the lowest in jar *A*. It is because in jar *A*, CO_2 released during respiration is used by the plant for the process of photosynthesis.
In jar *B*, the CO_2 is continuously released by the rats. So, its amount will remain same.
In jar *C*, CO_2 released by rats is not used up at all as there is no plant.

Q. 17 Observe the figure carefully and answer the following questions.

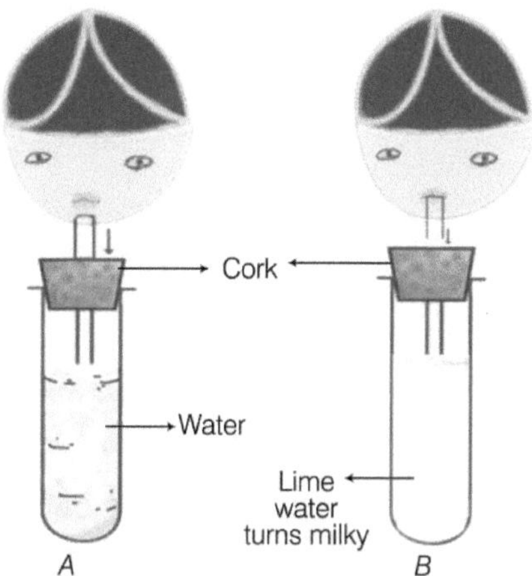

(a) Which process is being tested in the activity?
(b) What is the result of the activity? Give reasons.

Ans. (a) **Exhalation,** a part of process of respiration is being tested in the activity.

(b) The lime water in test tube *B* turns milky, but water in test tube *A* remains unchanged. Because CO_2 present in the exhaled air, mixes with lime water in test tube *B* and turns it milky.

Q. 18 A food stall owner was preparing dough for making bhaturas. He added a pinch of yeast and sugar to the dough and left it in a warm place. After few hours, the dough had risen. There was a sour smell too.

(a) Why did the dough rise?
(b) Why did the dough smell sour?
(c) Why was sugar added to the dough?
(d) What would have happened if the dough was kept in the refrigerator, soon after it was prepared?

Ans. (a) The dough rose due to the release of carbon dioxide during anaerobic respiration by the yeast.

(b) Yeast, during anaerobic respiration also produces alcohol which results in the sour smell of dough.

(c) Sugar is added into the dough, because it acts as a food for yeast. Yeast on incomplete breakdown of sugar or food produces CO_2, alcohol and energy (in less amount).

(d) If the dough was kept in the refrigerator soon after it was prepared, then dough will neither rise nor become sour. Yeast requires high temperature to grow, multiply and to respire. At low temperature, the yeast will not multiply or respire and therefore, no CO_2 or alcohol would be formed.

Q. 19 Observe the given figures labelled as *A* and *B* and answer the following questions.

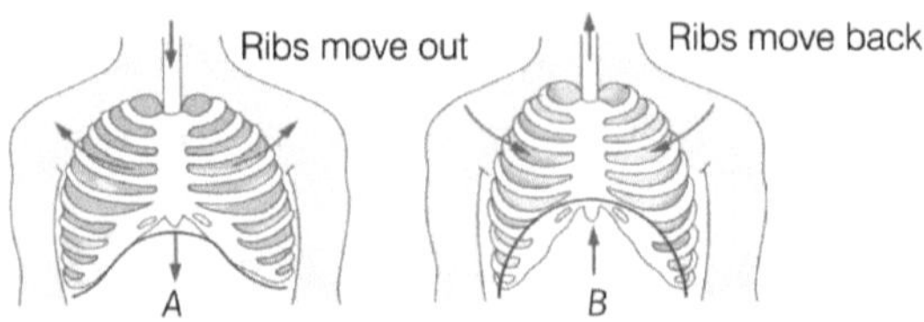

(a) Which of the figures, *A* or *B* indicates the process of inhalation and which shows the process of exhalation?

(b) In the figure label the arrows and indicate the direction of

(i) movement of air

(ii) movement of diaphragm

(iii) movement of ribs.

Ans. (a) Figure *A* indicates inhalation and figure *B* indicates exhalation. During inhalation, the ribs contract to move outward and upward, while during exhalation, the movement reverses, i.e. ribs relaxes to move inward and downward.

(b) Movement of air, diaphragm and ribs are indicated in below figures:

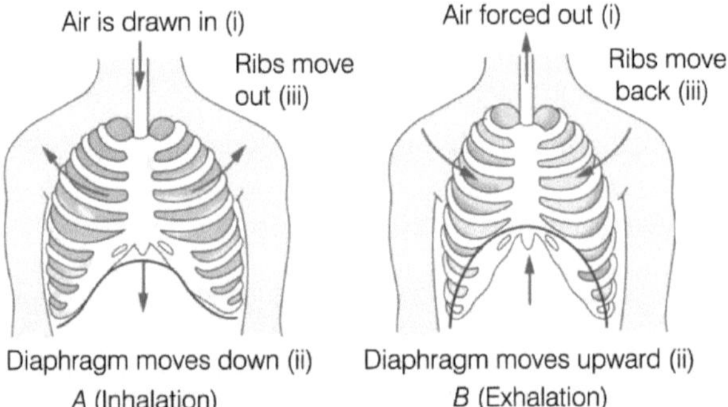

A (Inhalation) *B* (Exhalation)

Q. 20 Match the names of organisms in column I with their organs of breathing given in column II.

	Column I		Column II
(a)	Butterfly	(i)	Lungs
(b)	Earthworm	(ii)	Gills
(c)	Sparrow	(iii)	Spiracles
(d)	Fish	(iv)	Skin

Ans. The correct matching is as given:

(a)—(iii), (b)—(iv), (c)—(i), (d)—(ii)

(a) Butterfly is an insect, that has openings called spiracles on the sides of its body for taking in oxygen rich air.

(b) Earthworm breathes through its most and slimy skin.

(c) Sparrow (i.e. bird) has lungs and numerous air sacs for circulation of air.

(d) Fish has gills that are well supplied with blood vessels to use oxygen dissolved in water.

11

Transportation in Animals and Plants

Multiple Choice Questions (MCQs)

Q. 1 The muscular tube through which stored urine is passed out of the body is called

(a) kidney (b) ureter (c) urethra (d) urinary bladder

Ans. *(c)* The urine formed in **kidneys** goes into the **urinary bladder** through the tubes called **ureters**. The urine collected in bladder passed out from the body at regular intervals through the opening at the end of a tube called **urethra**.

Q. 2 They are pipe-like consisting of a group of specialised cells. They transport substances and form a two-way traffic in plants. Which of the following terms qualifies for the features mentioned above?

(a) Xylem tissue (b) Vascular tissue (c) Root hairs (d) Phloem tissue

Ans. *(d)* The vascular tissue called **phloem** forms a two-way traffic in plants for transport of substances. It carries the food from leaves to all other parts of plant.

The other options, i.e. **xylem tissue** carries water from the roots upwards to stem and leaves, **vascular tissue** consists of xylem and phloem vessels in plants and **root hairs** absorb water from the soil that moves from cell to cell in the root and ultimately enters the xylem vessels.

Q. 3 The absorption of nutrients and exchange of respiratory gases between blood and tissues takes place in

(a) veins (b) arteries (c) heart (d) capillaries

Ans. *(d)* **Capillaries** are the extremely thin blood vessels where exchange of substances and absorption of nutrients take place. Their thin walls facilitate the exchange.

They connect **arteries** (carry oxygenated blood from the heart) to **veins** (carry deoxygenated blood from all the parts of body to the heart).

Q. 4 In which of the following parts of human body are sweat glands absent?

(a) Scalp (b) Armpits (c) Lips (d) Palms

Ans. *(c)* Sweat glands are absent in lips.

These glands produce a liquid waste called sweat that contains water, salts and little urea. These are found over most of the body part.

Q. 5 In a tall tree which force is responsible for pulling water and minerals from the soil?

(a) Gravitational force
(b) Transportation force
(c) Suction force
(d) Conduction force

Ans. *(c)* In a tall tree, suction force is generated by continuous evaporation of water (transpiration), that pulls up water and minerals absorbed by the roots from the soil to reach the leaves.

Q. 6 Aquatic animals like fish excrete their wastes in gaseous form as

(a) oxygen
(b) hydrogen
(c) ammonia
(d) nitrogen

Ans. *(c)* The way in which waste product are excreted from the body of an animal depends on the availability of water to it. Aquatic animals live in water, so they excrete cell waste in gaseous form as ammonia which directly dissolves in water.

Very Short Answer Type Questions

Q. 7 Veins have valves which allow blood to flow only in one direction. Arteries do not have valves. Yet the blood flows in one direction only. Can you explain why?

Ans. Veins have valves to prevent blood from flowing backwards. Arteries also carry blood only in one direction but they do not have valves.

This is because the blood flows through them at high pressure. Their thick and elastic walls can withstand the high pressure of blood.

Q. 8 What is the special feature present in a human heart which does not allow mixing of blood when oxygen rich and carbon dioxide rich blood reach the heart?

Ans. In human, the heart has four chambers. The two upper chambers are called the **atria** and the two lower chambers are called the **ventricles**.

On the left side are the left atrium and left ventricle and on the right side of the heart are right atrium and right ventricle.

The left side of the heart is completely separated from its right side by means fo a partition of thick muscles called the **septum**. This septum prevents the mixing of oxygenated blood on the left side with the deoxygenated blood on its right side.

Q. 9 Name the organ which is located in the chest cavity with its lower tip slightly tilted towards the left.

Ans. The **heart** is the organ located in the chest cavity with its lower tip slightly tilted towards the left. It is roughly the size of a fist and beats continuosly to act as pump for the transport of blood.

Short Answer Type Questions

Q. 10 Look at figure and draw another figure of the same set-up as would be observed after a few hours.

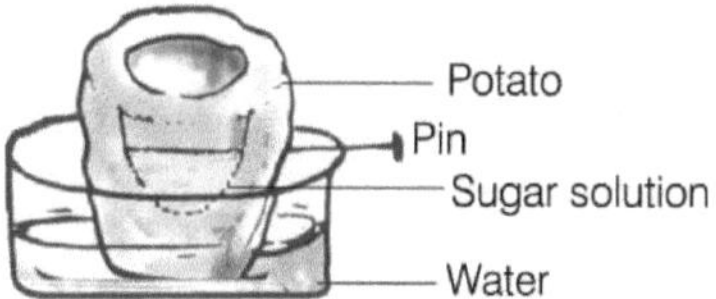

Ans. After a few hours, the same set-up would be as shown as below:

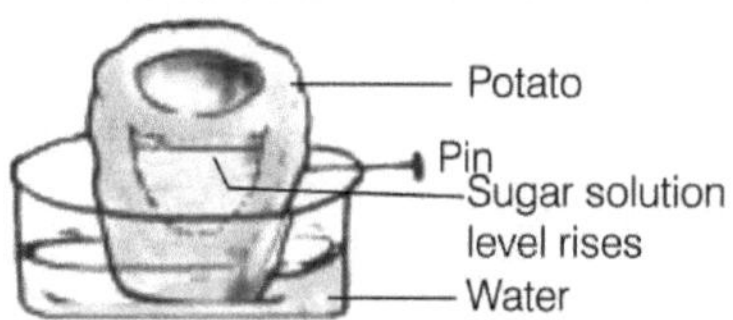

This figure shows that there will be an increase in the level of sugar solution in the potato piece. The level of sugar solution can rise only if some water from the petridish passes through the wall of potato and goes inside it.

Since, the water level has risen, it shows that water can move from cell to cell in the potato wall and reaches inside the cavity.

Q. 11 Arrange the following statements in the correct order in which they occur during the formation and removal of urine in human beings.

(a) Ureters carry urine to the urinary bladder.

(b) Wastes dissolved in water are filtered out as urine in the kidneys.

(c) Urine stored in urinary bladder is passed out through the urinary opening at the end of the urethra.

(d) Blood containing useful and harmful substances reaches the kidneys for filtration.

(e) Useful substances are absorbed back into the blood.

Ans. The correct order of the formation and removal of urine in human beings is

(d) Blood containing useful and harmful substances reaches the kidneys for filtration.

(e) Useful substances are absorbed back into the blood.

(b) Wastes dissolved in water is filtered out as urine in the kidneys.

(a) Ureters carry urine to the urinary bladder.

(c) Urine stored in urinary bladder is passed out through the urinary opening at the end of the urethra.

Q. 12 Paheli uprooted a rose plant from the soil. Most of the root tips, with root hairs got left behind in the soil. She planted it in a pot with new soil and watered it regularly. Will the plant grow or die? Give reason for your answer.

Ans. Possible answers are:

(i) Without the root hairs, the roots will not be able to absorb water and nutrients and the plant will die.

(ii) The stem of the rose plant may grow new roots and the plant will live.

(iii) The rose plant may not be able to survive in a different type of soil.

Q. 13 (a) Name the only artery that carries carbon dioxide rich blood.

(b) Why is it called an artery if it does not carry oxygen-rich blood?

Ans. (a) The only artery that carries carbon dioxide rich blood is **pulmonary artery**. It carries deoxygenated blood from the right ventricle of the heart to the lungs.

(b) The main function of artery is to carry blood away from the heart. Also, arteries have thick walls and do not contain valves. Blood flow in arteries, takes place at high pressure. All these characteristics are found in pulmonary artery. It carries away deoxygenated blood from heart to lungs for oxygenation, therefore it is called an artery.

Q. 14 Boojho's uncle was hospitalised and put on dialysis after a severe infection in both of his kidneys.

(a) What is dialysis?

(b) When does it become necessary to take such a treatment?

Ans. (a) Dialysis is the process of filtering blood periodically for removing wastes through an artificial kidney.

(b) It becomes necessary to take such a treatment when there is complete failure of both the kidneys. In such cases, accumulation of urea in the person's blood takes place. This can ultimately kill the person if the blood is not filtered artificially.

Q. 15 Name the process and the organ which helps in removing the following wastes from the body.

(a) Carbon dioxide
(b) Undigested food
(c) Urine
(d) Sweat

Ans. The process, waste and the organ involved in removal are as given below:

	Waste	Process	Organ
(a)	Carbon dioxide	Exhalation	Lungs
(b)	Undigested food	Egestion	Large intestine and anus
(c)	Urine	Excretion	Kidneys
(d)	Sweat	Perspiration (sweating)	Sweat glands

Q. 16 Observe the figure and answer the given questions:

(a) Name the instrument.

(b) Label the parts *A*, *B* and *C*.

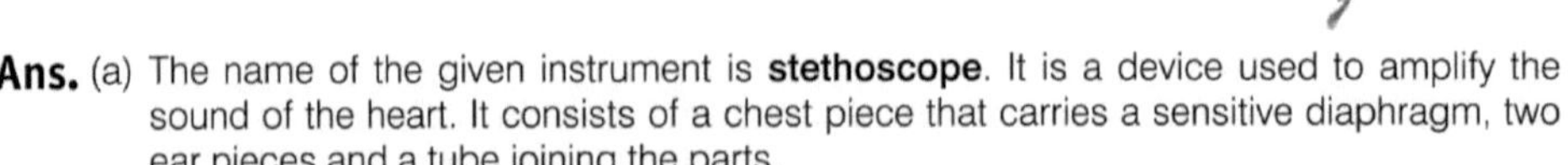

Ans. (a) The name of the given instrument is **stethoscope**. It is a device used to amplify the sound of the heart. It consists of a chest piece that carries a sensitive diaphragm, two ear pieces and a tube joining the parts.

(b) Labelled diagram of stethoscope.

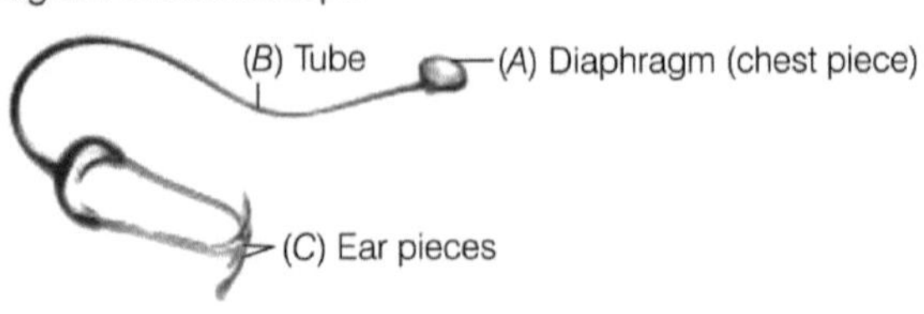

Q. 17 Paheli noticed water being pulled up by a motor pump to an overhead tank of a five storeyed building. She wondered how water moves up to great heights in the tall trees standing next to the building. Can you tell how?

Ans. When the water is pulled up by a motor-pump to an overhead tank of a five storeyed building, it moves to a great height due to the **suction pull** created by the pump. This pull forms a continuous column of water and water rises up to a great height.

Similarly, when **transpiration** occurs in the leaves of a tall tree, water is evaporated through the pores called stomata. The continuous evaporation creates a suction force.

Due to this suction force, water from the soil rises up through the roots of the plants and reaches to a great height in tall trees.

Long Answer Type Questions

Q. 18 Match the parts of the heart in column I with the direction of flow of blood in column II.

	Column I		Column II
(a)	Right ventricle	(i)	Pushes blood into the pulmonary artery.
(b)	Pulmonary veins	(ii)	Take deoxygenated blood from the heart to lungs.
(c)	Left atrium	(iii)	Receives blood from different parts of the body.
(d)	Pulmonary arteries	(iv)	Bring oxygenated blood from lungs to the heart.
(e)	Left ventricle	(v)	Pushes blood into the aorta.
(f)	Right auricle	(vi)	Receives oxygenated blood from the pulmonary veins.

Ans. The correct matching is as given:

(a)—(i), (b)—(iv), (c)—(vi), (d)—(ii), (e)—(v), (f)—(iii)

Q. 19 Read the following terms given below.

Root hairs	Xylem	Urethra
Arteries	Kidneys	Veins
Atria	Capillaries	Heart
Ureter	Phloem	Urinary bladder

Group the terms on the basis of the categories given below.

(a) Circulatory system of animals.
(b) Excretory system in human.
(c) Transport of substances in plants

Ans. The terms on the basis of the categories mentioned above can be grouped as follows:

(a) **Circulatory system of human** Arteries, atria, capillaries, veins, heart.

In the circulatory system, the **heart** (consists of two **atria** and two **ventricles**) acts as a pump to put out blood. The blood vessels (arteries, veins and capillaries) act as tubes through which blood flows in the whole body.

(b) **Excretory system in human** Urethra, kidneys, ureter and urinary bladder.

The excretory system of human consists of two bean-shaped **kidneys** that filter blood to form urine. Urine goes into the **urinary bladder** through tubes called **ureters**. It goes out from body through the opening at the end of a tube called **urethra**.

(c) **Transport of substances in plants** Root hairs, xylem and phloem.

Transport system in plants consists of xylem and phloem. The water absorbed by root hairs from soil reaches xylem to move upward to stem, branches and leaves. Phloem carries food from leaves to other parts.

Q. 20 Fill in the blanks of the following paragraph using just two words, arteries and veins.

......(a)...... carry oxygen rich blood from the heart to all parts of the body and ......(b)...... carry carbon dioxide rich blood from all parts of the body back to the heart. ......(c)...... have thin walls and ......(d)...... have thick elastic walls. Blood flows at high pressure in ......(e)...... . Valves are present in ......(f)...... which allow blood to flow only towards the heart. ......(g)...... divide into smaller vessels. These vessels further divide into extremely thin tubes called capillaries. The capillaries join up to form ......(h)...... .

Ans. (a) Arteries (b) veins
(c) Veins (d) arteries
(e) arteries (f) veins
(g) Arteries (h) veins

Q. 21 While learning to ride a bicycle, Boojho lost his balance and fell. He got bruises on his knees and it started bleeding. However, the bleeding stopped after sometime.

(a) Why did the bleeding stop?
(b) What would be the colour of the wounded area and why?
(c) Which type of blood cells are responsible for clotting of blood?

Ans. (a) A wound stops bleeding after sometime due to the process of **clot formation**. It plugs the cut and bleeding stops.

(b) Wounded area becomes dark red in colour due to the clotting of blood.

(c) The blood clot is formed due to the presence of the cells called **platelets** in the blood.

12

Reproduction in Plants

Multiple Choice Questions (MCQs)

Q. 1 Which of the following parts of a plant take part in sexual reproduction?

(i) Flower (ii) Seed
(iii) Fruit (iv) Branch

Choose the correct answer from below

(a) (i) and (ii) (b) (i), (ii) and (iii)
(c) (iii) and (iv) (d) (ii), (iii) and (iv)

Ans. *(b)* The **flowers** perform the function of sexual reproduction in plant. After fertilisation, the ovary grows into a **fruit** and **seeds** develop from the ovules.

Q. 2 Lila observed that a pond with clear water was covered up with a green algae within a week. By which method of reproduction did the algae spread so rapidly?

(a) Budding
(b) Sexual reproduction
(c) Fragmentation
(d) Pollination

Ans.*(c)* In the presence of water and nutrients, algae grow and multiply rapidly by fragmentation. An alga breaks up into two or more fragments, each of which grow into new individuals. This process cover a large area in a short period of time.

Q. 3 Seeds of drumstick and maple are carried to long distances by wind because they possess

(a) winged seeds
(b) large and hairy seeds
(c) long and ridged fruits
(d) spiny seeds

Ans. *(a)* Seeds of drumstick and maple have wings which help them to be easily carried away by wind. Various seeds and fruits have some special feature due to which they are carried away in a particular way (by wind, water or animal).

Q. 4 The 'eye' of the potato plant is what

(a) the root is to any plant
(b) the bud is to a flower
(c) the bud is to *Bryophyllum* leaf
(d) the anther is to stamen

Ans. ***(c)*** The eye of the potato is the same as the bud is to *Bryophyllum* leaf. Both the structures are vegetative propagules. They can form a new plant from them. This method of asexual reproduction through the vegetative parts of the existing plant is called vegetative propagation.

Q. 5 The ovaries of different flowers may contain

(a) only one ovule
(b) many ovules
(c) one to many ovules
(d) only two ovules

Ans. ***(c)*** Ovary is the part of female reproductive organ of the plant (i.e. pistil). It may contain one or many ovules in different flowers. The ovule in turn contains the female gamete of egg.

Q. 6 Which of the following statements is/are true for sexual reproduction in plants?

(i) Plants are obtained from seeds
(ii) Two plants are always essential
(iii) Fertilisation can occur only after pollination
(iv) Only insects are agents of pollination

Choose from the options given below

(a) (i) and (ii)
(b) only (i)
(c) (ii) and (iii)
(d) (i) and (iv)

Ans. ***(a)*** Statements (i) and (ii) are correct.

A seed on germination grows into a new plant and fertilisation in plants can only occur after pollination (i.e. only when pollen grains have fallen on the stigma of flower).

Other statements are incorrect as a plant bearing bisexual flowers can undergo sexual reproduction itself as both male and female reproductive organs are present. Also, along with insects, wind and water are also agents of pollination.

Q. 7 Pollination refers to the

(a) transfer of pollen from anther to ovary
(b) transfer of male gametes from anther to stigma
(c) transfer of pollen from anther to stigma
(d) transfer of pollen from anther to ovule

Ans. ***(c)*** The transfer of pollen grains from anther of a stamen to stigma of a pistil is called **pollination**. It can occur by two ways as self-pollination (transfer occur in same flower or another flower of same plant) and cross-pollination (transfer occurring between flowers of two separate but similar plants. Insects, water and wind are agents of pollination.

Very Short Answer Type Questions

Q. 8 Fungus, moss and fern reproduce by a common method of asexual reproduction. Name the method.

Ans. Fungus, moss and fern reproduce by the method of **spore formation**, which is a type of asexual reproduction. Spores are asexual reproductive bodies produced by the parent plant, in spore cases.

When the spore cases burst, the spores with hard protective layer are spread into air.

On return of favourable conditions, the spores germinate and produce new plants.

Q. 9 Pick the odd one out from the following on the basis of mode of reproduction and give reason for it,
Sugarcane, Potato, Rice, Rose.

Ans. The odd one out is rice. As it reproduces by sexual reproduction. All the other three, i.e. sugarcane, potato and rose reproduce through vegetative propagation.

Q. 10 Boojho had the following parts of a rose plant–a leaf, roots, a branch, a flower, a bud and pollen grains. Which of them can be used to grow a new rose plant?

Ans. The branch can be used to grow a new rose plant, as rose reproduces through vegetative propagation by stem cutting method. The lower end of the stem cutting is buried in soil and the upper part having the bud is kept above the ground. The planted cutting is watered everyday.

After a few days, the cutting in soil develops roots and bud produces a shoot. In this way a branch cutting of a rose plant grows to become a new rose plant.

Q. 11 Which type of pollination does the given figure indicate?

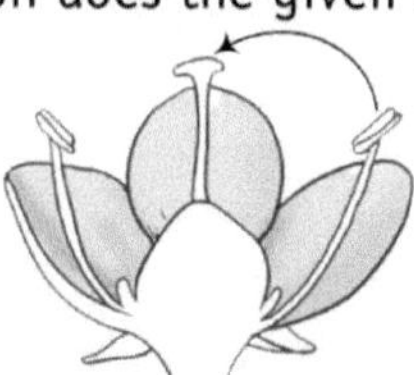

Ans. The given figure shows **self-pollination**, as the pollen grains from anther of the flower are transferred to the stigma of same flower.

Q. 12 One morning as Paheli strolled in her garden she noticed many small plants, which were not there a week ago. She wondered, where they had come from as nobody had planted them there. Explain the reason for the growth of these plants.

Ans. The small plants which were not there in the garden a weak ago may have grown up due to the seed dispersal. The seeds from the tree may have fallen below or have been dispersed by wind or animals on the ground, which on germination developed into new small plants.

Short Answer Type Questions

Q. 13 In the figure given below, label the part marked (i), (ii) and (iii).

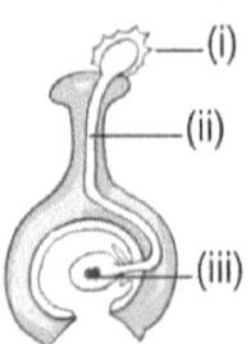

Ans. The parts in the given figure can be labelled as follows:

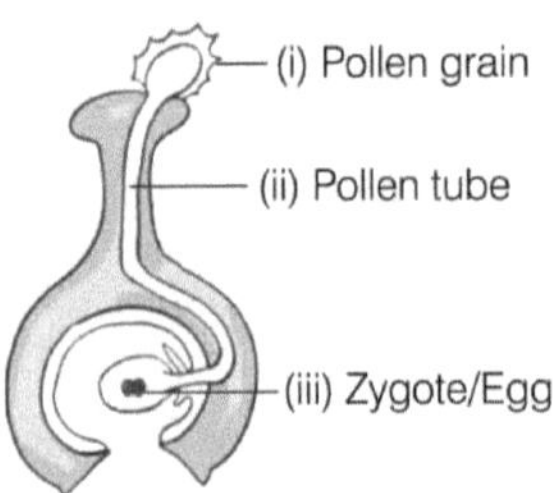

When a **pollen grain** falls on the stigma of a flower, it grows into a **pollen tube** downwards through the style towards the **egg** in ovary. A male gamete moves down the **pollen tube** and fuses with female gamete in ovary to form a **zygote**.

Q. 14 When you keep food items like bread and fruits outside for a long time especially during the rainy season, you will observe a cottony growth on them.

(a) What is this growth called?

(b) How does the growth take place?

Ans. (a) When food items like bread and fruits are kept outside for a long time especially during rainy season, a cottony growth of **bread mould** (a fungus) is observed.

(b) The growth of fungus takes place by spores present in air, which when comes in contact with moisture on bread germinates and grow to produce new cells.

Q. 15 Group the seeds given in figure (i) to (iii) according to their means of dispersion.

(a) Seed dispersed by wind.

(b) Seed dispersed by water.

(c) Seed dispersed by animal.

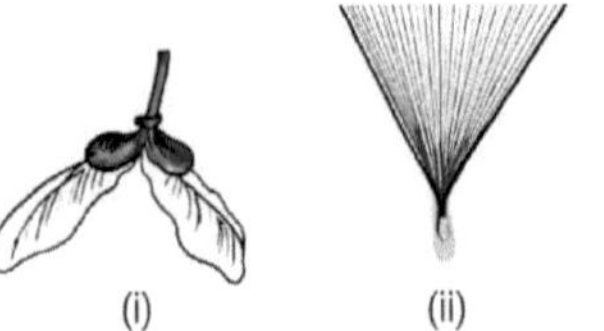

Ans. The seeds and their means of dispersal are:

(a) **Seed dispersed by wind** The seed of maple (i) (winged seed which are light in weight) and seed of aak or madar (ii) (hairy outgrowth, which makes it lighter) can be dispersed by wind.

(b) **Seed dispersed by water** Seeds having spongy form and floating ability which are dispersed by water to different places.

(c) **Seed dispersed by animals** Seed of *Xanthium* (iii) are spiny with on them which gets attached to the bodies of animals and are carried to distant places.

None of the seed given in the figure is dispersed by water.

Q. 16 Coconut is a large and heavy fruit. How is it adapted for dispersal by water?

Ans. The coconut fruits have a very developed fibrous outer coat which enables them to float in water. They are thus carried away by flowing water to distant places.

Long Answer Type Questions

Q. 17 In the figure of a flower given under, label the parts whose functions are given below and give their names.

(a) The part which contains pollen grains.
(b) The part where the female gamete is formed.
(c) The female reproductive part, where pollen grains germinate.
(d) The colourful part of flower which attracts insects.

Ans. The various parts of a flower whose functions are mentioned above are labelled as follows:

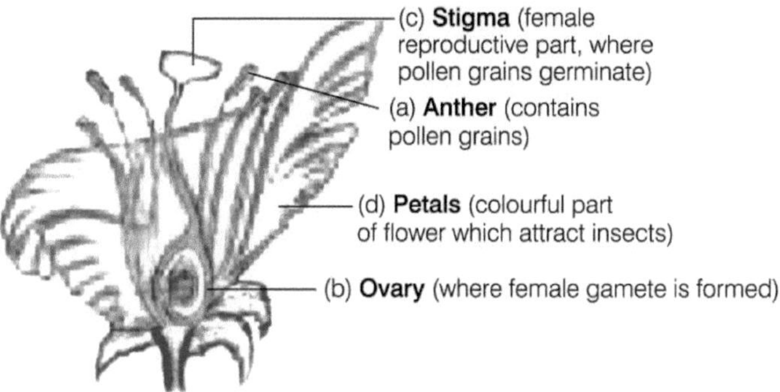

Q. 18 Fill in the blanks with correct terms. The male and female gametes fuse to form a ...(a)... during the process of ...(b)... . This grows into an ...(c)... which is enclosed within a seed. After fertilisation the ovules develop into ...(d)... and the ovary develops into a ...(e)... .

Ans. (a) zygote
(b) fertilisation
(c) embryo
(d) seed
(e) fruit

Q. 19 In the diagram of a bisexual flower given as figure draw the missing part and label the parts marked (a), (b) and (c). Also label the missing part that you draw.

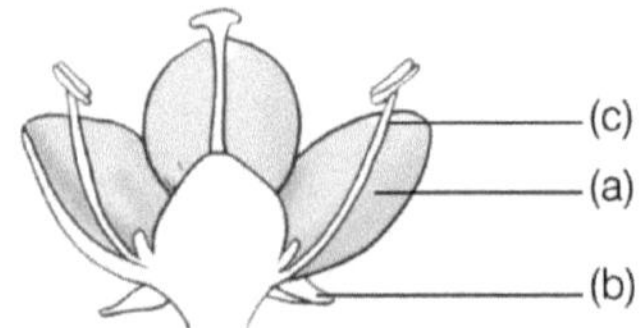

Ans. The missing part along with the labelled part is as follows:

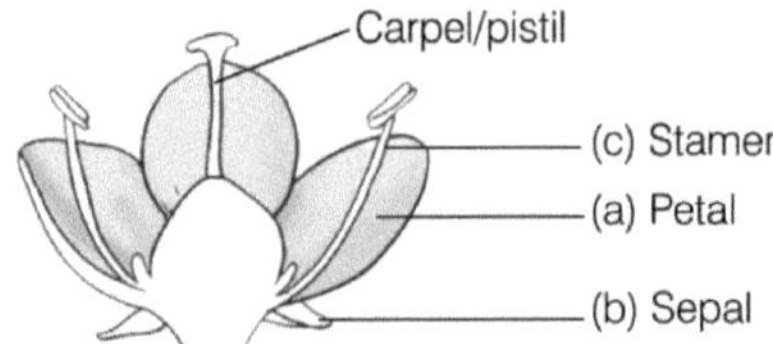

Q. 20 Write how the following seeds are dispersed.
(a) Seeds with wings
(b) Small and light seeds
(c) Seeds with spines/hooks

Ans. The mode of dispersal of the seeds with their characteristic properties are as follows:

(a) **Seeds with wings**, e.g. Seeds of drumstick and maple are light weighted and can be blown away by air. Thus, these are dispersed by **wind**.

(b) **Small and light seeds**, e.g. Seeds of grasses and cotton (having hairy growth) are also dispersed through wind.

(c) Seeds with spines/hooks, e.g. Seeds of *Xanthium*, *Urena*, the hooks or spines of seeds attach to the animal body. When animals move to other places and rub their body with tree, etc. These seeds fall from their body and get dispersed. Therefore, these are dispersed through **animals**.

13

Motion and Time

Multiple Choice Questions (MCQs)

Q. 1 Which of the following cannot be used for the measurement of time?

(a) A leaking tap
(b) Simple pendulum
(c) Shadow of an object during the day
(d) Blinking of eyes

Ans. *(d)* Blinking of eyes is not a periodic phenomenon (i.e. it does not repeat after definite intervals of time), so we cannot measure the time using this phenomenon.

Q. 2 Two clocks *A* and *B* are shown in figure. Clock *A* has an hour and a minute hand whereas clock *B* has an hour hand, minute hand as well as a second hand. Which of the following statement is correct for these clocks?

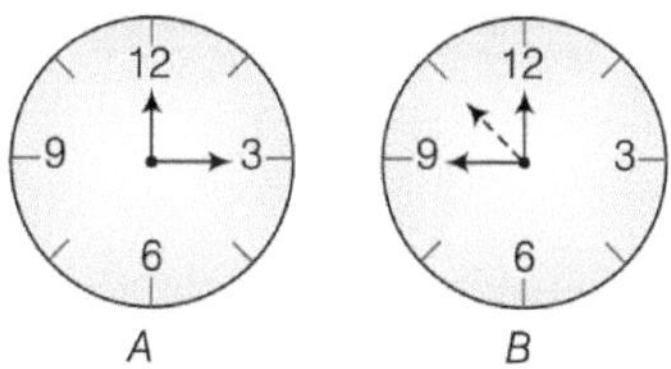

(a) A time interval of 30 seconds can be measured by clock *A*
(b) A time interval of 30 seconds cannot be measured by clock *B*
(c) Time interval of 5 minutes can be measured by both *A* and *B*
(d) Time interval of 4 minutes 10 seconds can be measured by clock *A*

Ans. *(c)* The time interval of 5 min can be measured by both *A* and *B*. Since, the time interval of 30 seconds cannot be measured by clock *A* and can be measured by clock *B*. Also, the time interval of 4 min 10 seconds cannot be measured by clock *A*, but can be measured by clock *B*.

Q. 3 Two students were asked to plot a distance-time graph for the motion described by Table *A* and Table *B*.

Table *A*

Distance moved (m)	0	10	20	30	40	50
Time (min)	0	2	4	6	8	10

Table B

Distance moved (m)	0	5	10	15	20	25
Time (min)	0	1	2	3	4	5

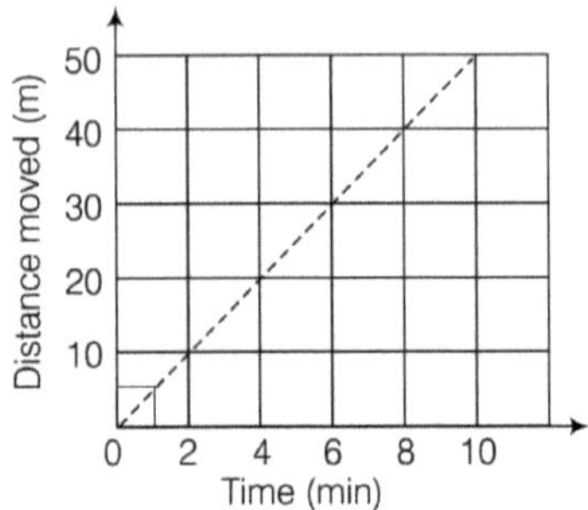

The graph given in figure is true for

(a) Both *A* and *B* (b) Only *A* (c) Only *B* (d) Neither *A* Nor *B*

Ans. ***(a)*** Since, speed is constant for *A* and *B*, so graph for *A* and *B* will be a straight line as given in figure.

Q. 4 A bus travels 54 km in 90 min. The speed of the bus is

(a) 0.6 m/s (b) 10 m/s (c) 5.4 m/s (d) 3.6 m/s

Ans. ***(b)*** As, we know that

$$\text{Speed} = \frac{\text{Distance}}{\text{Time}} = \frac{54 \times 1000}{90 \times 60} = 10\,\text{m/s} \quad \left[\begin{array}{l}\because 1\text{ km} = 1000\text{ m} \\ \because 1\text{min} = 60\text{ s}\end{array}\right]$$

Q. 5 If we denote speed by *S*, distance by *D* and time by *T*, the relationship between these quantities is

(a) $S = D \times T$ (b) $T = \frac{S}{D}$ (c) $S = \frac{1}{T} \times D$ (d) $S = \frac{T}{D}$

Ans. ***(c)*** The correct relationship is $S = \frac{1}{T} \times D.$ $\left[\because \text{Speed } (S) = \frac{\text{Distance } (D)}{\text{Time } (T)}\right]$

Q. 6 Observe the given figure.

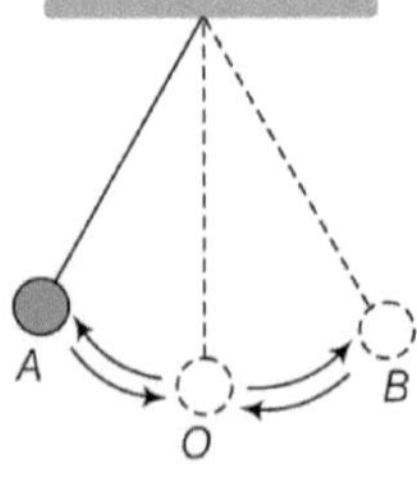

The time period of a simple pendulum is the time taken by it to travel from

(a) *A* to *B* and back to *A*
(b) *O* to *A*, *A* to *B* and *B* to *A*
(c) *B* to *A*, *A* to *B* and *B* to *O*
(d) *A* to *B*

Ans. ***(a)*** Time period of a simple pendulum is the total time taken to complete one full cycle. (i.e. from *A* to *B* and back to *A*).

Q. 7 Figure shows an oscillating pendulum. Time taken by the bob to move from A to C is t_1 and from C to O is t_2. The time period of this simple pendulum is

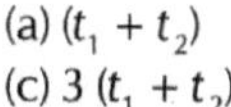

(a) $(t_1 + t_2)$ (b) $2(t_1 + t_2)$
(c) $3(t_1 + t_2)$ (d) $4(t_1 + t_2)$

Ans. ***(d)*** The total time taken by the bob to move from A to O is $(t_1 + t_2)$, which is $\frac{1}{4}$ th time of one full cycle of pendulum. Time period of pendulum i.e. time taken by pendulum to complete one oscillation from A to B and back to A will be $4(t_1 + t_2)$.

Q. 8 The correct symbol to represent the speed of an object is

(a) 5 m/s (b) 5 mp (c) 5 m/s^{-1} (d) 5 s/m

Ans. ***(a)*** 5 m/s is the correct symbol to represent the speed of an object because the unit of speed is m/s (or ms^{-1}).

Q. 9 Boojho walks to his school which is at a distance of 3 km from his home in 30 min. On reaching, he finds that the school is closed and comes back by a bicycle with his friend and reaches home in 20 min. His average speed in km/h is

(a) 8.3 (b) 7.2 (c) 5 (d) 3.6

Ans. ***(b)*** Given, total distance $= 3 + 3 = 6$ km, total time $= 30 + 20 = 50 \text{ min} = \frac{50}{60}$ h

$$\text{Average speed} = \frac{\text{Total distance}}{\text{Total time taken}} = \frac{6}{\frac{50}{60}} = \frac{6}{50} \times 60 = 7.2 \text{ km/h} \quad [\because 1\text{h} = 60 \text{ min}]$$

Very Short Answer Type Questions

Q. 10 A simple pendulum is oscillating between two points A and B as shown in figure. Is the motion of the bob uniform or non-uniform?

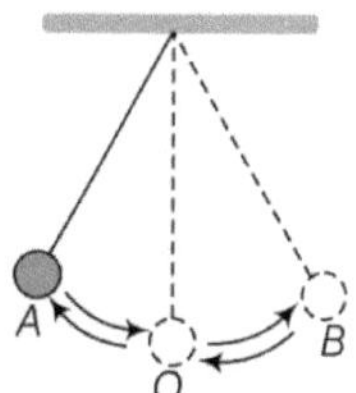

Ans. The motion of bob is non-uniform, as it does not cover equal distance in equal intervals of time.

Q. 11 Paheli and Boojho have to cover different distances to reach their school but they take the same time to reach the school. What can you say about their speed?

Ans. They do not have equal speed because they cover unequal distances in equal intervals of time. One of them has higher speed, whom has to cover larger distance with respect to other.

Q. 12 If Boojho covers a certain distance in one hour and Paheli covers the same distance in two hours, who travels in a higher speed?

Ans. Boojho travels with a higher speed, as he has covered the same distance in lesser time than Paheli.

Short Answer Type Questions

Q. 13 Complete the data of the table given below with the help of the distance-time graph given in figure.

Distance (m)	0	4	?	12	?	20
Time (s)	0	2	4	?	8	10

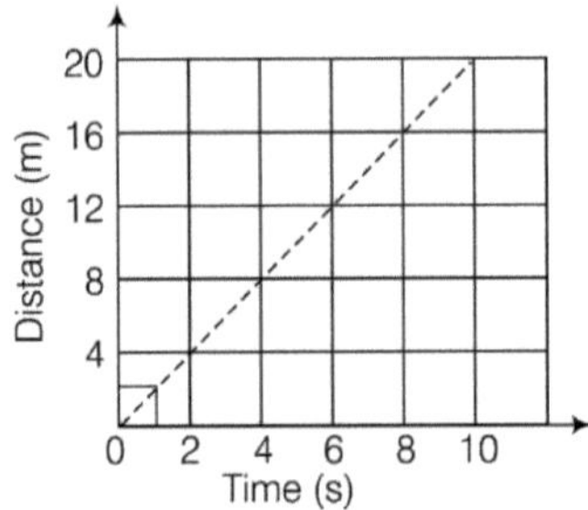

Ans. From the graph given above, it is a case of uniform motion, so

Distance (m)	0	4	8	12	16	20
Time (s)	0	2	4	6	8	10

Q. 14 The average age of children of class VII is 12 years and 3 months. Express this age in seconds.

Ans. Given, the average age of children is 12 years and 3 months

$$1 \text{ year} = 365 \text{ days} = 365 \times 24 \text{ h} \quad [\because 1 \text{ day} = 24 \text{ h}]$$

$$= 365 \times 24 \times 3600 \text{ s} = 31536000 \text{ s} \quad [\because 1 \text{ h} = 3600 \text{ s}]$$

$\therefore$ 12 years $= 31536000 \text{ s} \times 12 = 378432000 \text{ s}$

and 3 months $= 3 \times 30$ days $= 30 \times 3 \times 24$ h $= 30 \times 3 \times 24 \times 3600$ s $= 7776000$ s

So, total age in second $= 378432000 + 7776000 = 386208000$ s

Q. 15 A spaceship travels 36000 km in one hour. Express its speed in km/s.

Ans. As, Speed $= \dfrac{\text{Distance}}{\text{Time}} = \dfrac{36000 \text{ km}}{1 \text{ h}} = \dfrac{36000}{1 \times 3600} = 10 \text{ km/s}$ $\quad [\because 1 \text{ h} = 3600 \text{ s}]$

Q. 16 Starting from *A*, Paheli moves along a rectangular path *ABCD* as shown in figure. She takes 2 min to travel each side. Plot a distance-time graph and explain whether the motion is uniform or non-uniform.

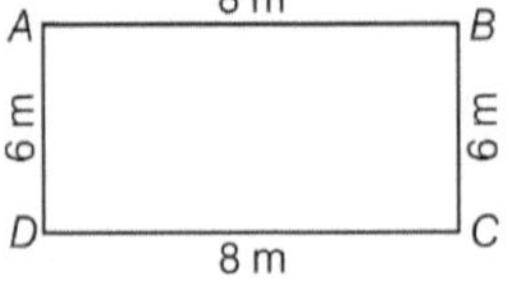

Ans. Since, the speed i.e., the distance covered per unit time for the entire distance covered is not the same, therefore, the motion is a non-uniform motion.

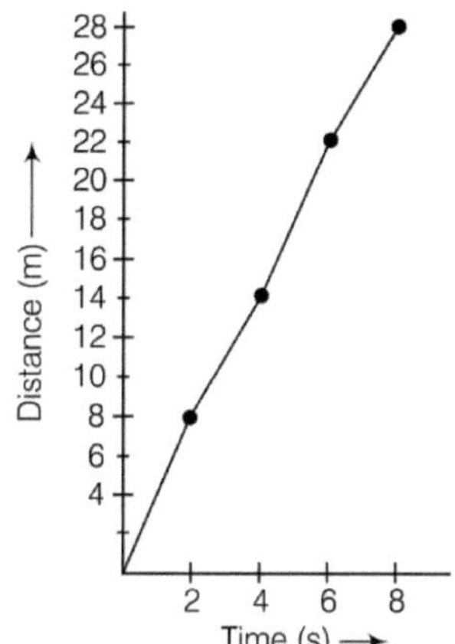

Q. 17 Plot a distance-time graph of the tip of the second hand of a clock by selecting 4 points on *X*-axis and *Y*-axis, respectively. The circumference of the circle traced by the second hand is 64 cm.

Ans. The circumference of circle traced by a second hand in 60 sec is 64 cm.

Time (s)	*X*	15	30	45	60
Distance (cm)	*Y*	16	32	48	64

Here, equal distance is covered in equal intervals of time.

So, graph will be a straight line.

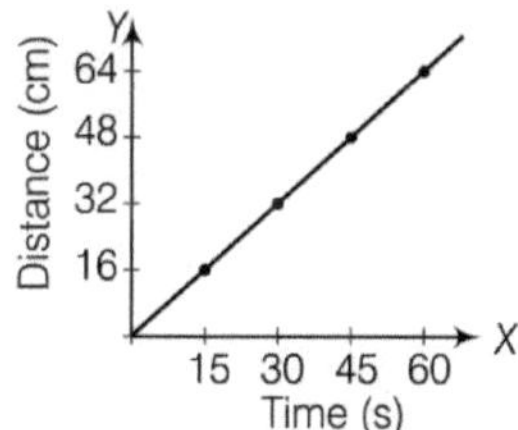

Long Answer Type Questions

Q. 18 Given below as figure is the distance-time graph of the motion of an object.

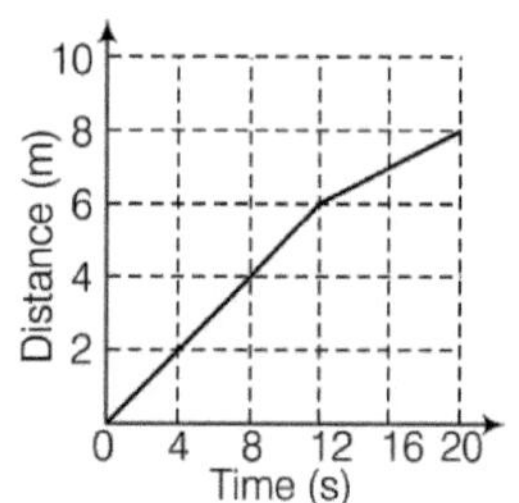

(a) What will be the position of the object at 20 s?

(b) What will be the distance travelled by the object in 12 s?

(c) What is the average speed of the object?

Ans. (a) From the graph, it is clear that the distance at 20 s is 8 m.

(b) Distance travelled by the object in 12 s is 6 m.

(c) Average speed $= \dfrac{\text{Total distance}}{\text{Total time}} = \dfrac{8}{20} = 0.4\ \text{m/s}$

Q. 19 Distance between Bholu's and Golu's house is 9 km. Bholu has to attend Golu's birthday party at 7 O' clock. He started his journey from his home at 6 O' clock on his bicycle and covered a distance of 6 km in 40 min. At that point, he met Chintu and he spoke to him for 5 min and reached Golu's birthday party at 7 O' clock. With what speed, did he cover the second part of the journey? Calculate his average speed for the entire journey.

Ans. From the question, Bholu covers the remaining 3 km distance in 15 min.

So, speed of Bholu $= \dfrac{\text{Distance}}{\text{Time}} = \dfrac{3\text{ km}}{\frac{15}{60}\text{h}} = \dfrac{3}{15} \times 60 = 12$ km/h $\left(\because 1 \text{ min} = \dfrac{1}{60}\text{ h}\right)$

Now, average speed $= \dfrac{\text{Total distance travelled}}{\text{Total time taken}} = \dfrac{9}{1} = 9$ km/h

Q. 20 Boojho goes to the football ground to play football. The distance-time graph of his journey from his home to the ground is given as figure.

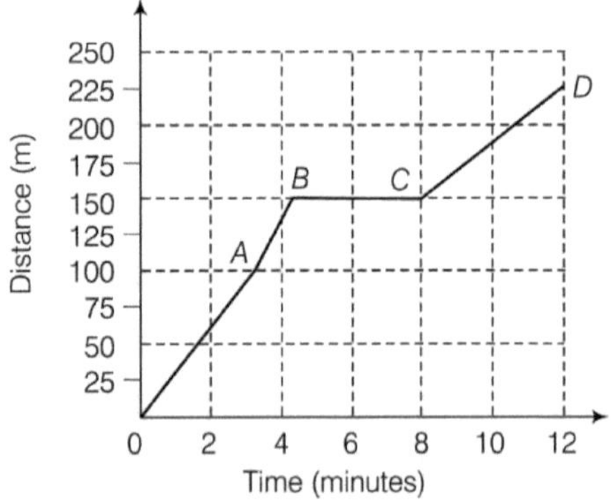

(a) What does the graph between points *B* and *C* indicate about the motion of Boojho?

(b) Is the motion between 0 to 4 min uniform or non-uniform?

(c) What is his speed between 8 and 12 minutes of his journey?

Ans. (a) Since, the graph between *B* and *C* is parallel to time-axis, so it indicates that Boojho is at rest i.e. his speed is zero.

(b) Since, the graph is not straight line, so it is a non-uniform motion.

(c) As, speed $= \dfrac{\text{Distance}}{\text{Time}} = \dfrac{225 - 150}{12 - 8} = \dfrac{75}{4} = 18.75$ m/min

14

Electric Current and Its Effects

Multiple Choice Questions (MCQs)

Q. 1 When an electric current flows through a copper wire *AB* as shown in figure, the wire

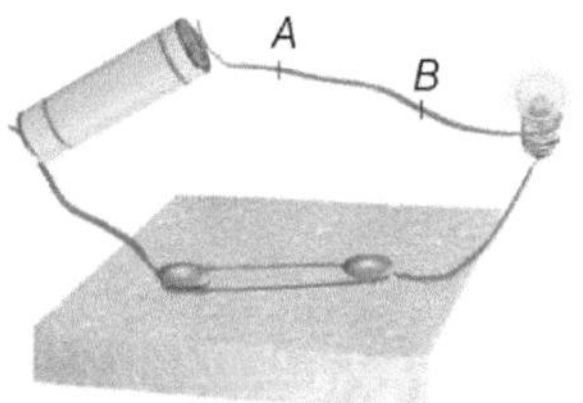

(a) deflects a magnetic needle placed near it
(b) becomes red hot
(c) gives electric shock
(d) behaves like a fuse

Ans. ***(a)*** It deflects a magnetic needle placed near it because a magnetic field is created when the current passes through it.

Q. 2 Choose the statement which is not correct in the case of an electric fuse.

(a) Fuses are inserted in electric circuits of all buildings.
(b) There is a maximum limit on the current which can safely flow through the electric circuits.
(c) There is a minimum limit on the current which can safely flow in the electric circuits.
(d) If a proper fuse is inserted in a circuit it will blow off if current exceeds the safe limit.

Ans. ***(c)*** In case of electric fuse, there is only a maximum limit on the current which can safely flow in the electric circuits.

Q. 3 Three bulbs A, B, C are connected in a circuit as shown in figure. When the switch is 'ON'

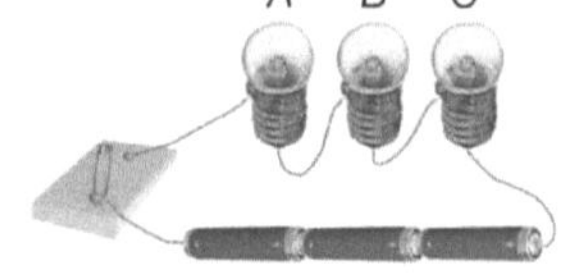

(a) bulb C will glow first.

(b) bulb B and C will glow simultaneously and bulb A will glow after some time.

(c) all the bulbs A,B and C will glow at the same time.

(d) The bulbs will glow in the order A, B and C.

Ans. *(c)* All the bulbs will glow simultaneously because there is no time lag in the flow of current as soon as the circuit is complete.

Q. 4 When a switch is in OFF position,

(i) circuit starting from positive terminal of the cell stops at the switch

(ii) circuit is open

(iii) no current flows through it

(iv) current flows after sometime

Choose the combination of correct answer from the following.

(a) All are correct
(b) (ii) and (iii) are correct
(c) Only (iv) is correct
(d) (i) and (ii) are correct

Ans. *(b)* When the switch is in OFF position, circuit is incomplete. It is said to be open and therefore, no current flows through it.

Q. 5 Which of the following precautions need not be taken while using electric gadgets/ appliances/circuit?

(a) We should never touch a lighted electric bulb connected to the mains.

(b) We should never do experiment with the electric supply from the mains or a generator or an inverter.

(c) We should never use just any wire or strip of metal in place of a fuse.

(d) We should never turn the switch in ON position.

Ans. *(d)* For using electric gadgets/ appliances/ circuit, we have to turn the switch in ON position. Therefore, precaution given in option (d) need not be considered.

Very Short Answer Type Questions

Q. 6 Which property of a conducting wire is utilised in making electric fuse?

Ans. Electric fuse wire is made from some special material which has low melting point. When large electric current is passed through a circuit, it melts quickly and breaks the circuit and prevents damages to electrical circuit.

Q. 7 Name device used these days in place of electric fuses in electrical circuits.

Ans. The device used these days in place of electric fuse is MCB (Miniature Circuit Breaker). This is a switch which automatically turns off when current in a circuit exceeds the safe limit.

Q. 8 Fill in the blanks:

(a) Our body is a .... of electricity.
(b) An electric cell produces electricity from the .... in it.
(c) In an electric circuit, a fuse is a .... to prevent possible fire.
(d) A combination of two or more cells is called a ....

Ans. (a) **Conductor** Our body is a good conductor of electricity as it allows the electric current to pass through it.

(b) **Chemicals** stored, an electric cell is a device capable of changing chemical energy into electrical energy (electricity).

(c) **Safety device** If by accident the current exceeds the safe limit, in a circuit, the fuse will blow off and break the circuit and will prevent damage to circuit and possible fire.

(d) **Battery** A combination of two or more cells, where the positive terminal of one cell is connected to the negative terminal of the next cell, is called a battery.

Q. 9 Unscramble the following words:

(a) TBTAYER (b) SFEU (c) HTRCO (d) HICWTS

Ans. (a) BATTERY It is a combination of two or more cells.

(b) FUSE It is a safety device in an electric circuit to prevent possible fire.

(c) TORCH It is a device portable lamp which uses battery for its operation.

(d) SWITCH It is an electric component which can make or break an electric circuit.

Q. 10 Paheli does not have a night lamp in her room. She covered the bulb of her room with a towel in the night to get dim light. Has she taken the right step? Give one reason to justify your answer.

Ans. No, she has not taken the right step. Because due to the excessive heat of bulb, the towel may burn and it will also result in the wastage of electrical energy.

Q. 11 Why are Compact Fluorescent Lamps (CFLs) preferred over electric bulbs?

Ans. CFLs are preferred over electric bulbs because electric bulbs use more power of electricity and losses electrical energy in the form of heat. However, CFLs do not waste electrical energy as heat.

Q. 12 Why is an electric fuse required in all electrical appliance?

Ans. Electric fuse is required in all electrical appliances to prevent damage from excessive current flow and during short circuit.

Short Answer Type Questions

Q. 13 Can we use the same fuse in a geyser and a television set? Explain.

Ans. No, we cannot use same fuse in a geyser and in a television set because the fuse used in every appliance has some limit to withstand the current flowing through it. So, different appliances have fuses of different ratings.

Q. 14 Name two electric devices for each where

(a) heating effect of current is used and
(b) magnetic effect of current is used.

Ans. (a) Heating effect of current is used in electric heater and geyser.

(b) Magnetic effect of current is used in electric bell and cranes to lift heavy magnetic materials from one place to other.

Q. 15 Why do we cover plug pinholes which are within the reach of children with cellotape or a plastic cover when not in use?

Ans. We do cover plug pinholes which are within the reach of children with cellotape or plastic cover to avoid electric shocks. If unconsciously, a child puts his finger into the electric socket, he/she may get a shock which could be fatal.

Q. 16 Boojho made an electromagnet by winding 50 turns of wire over an iron screw. Paheli also made an electromagnet by winding 100 turns over a similar iron screw. Which electromagnet will attract more pins? Give reason.

Ans. Since, the magnetic effect directly depends on the number of turns of wire on electromagnet. So, electromagnet of Paheli will attract more pins as it has more number of turns of wire on it and thus, it is a stronger electromagnet.

Q. 17 Your teacher has shown you the following activity.

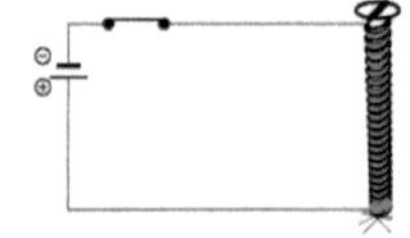

Activity: Teacher has wound a long insulated piece of wire around and iron nail in the form of a coil. Free ends of the wire are connected to a cell through a switch as shown in the figure. The current is switched on and some pins are placed near the ends of the nail.

Write down any three questions that come to your mind about this activity.

Ans. Some of the questions which may arise in our mind are as follows:

(i) Why does the iron nail attract the pins placed near its ends?

(ii) On disconnecting the circuit, why pins get detached from the iron nail?

(iii) What will happen if we use some other material like wood or straw in place of iron nail?

Q. 18 Paheli took a wire of length 10 cm. Boojho took a wire of 5 cm of the same material and thickness. Both of them connected with wires as shown in the circuit given in figure. The current flowing in both the circuits is the same.

(a) Will the heat produced in both the cases be equal? Explain.

(b) Will the heat produced be the same, if the wires taken by them are of equal lengths but of different thickness? Explain.

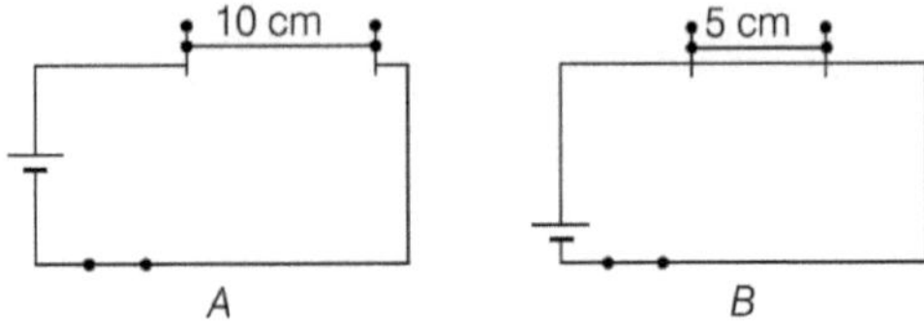

Ans. (a) No, the amount of heat produced in both the wires will be different because amount of heat produced in a wire on passing electric current depends upon the length of wire and here length is different for both the wires.

(b) No, the amount of heat produced in the wires of same lengths but different thickness cannot be the same because amount of heat produced in a wire depends upon the thickness of the wire.

Q. 19 How does the magnetic effect of electric current help in the working of an electric bell? Explain with the help of a diagram.

Ans. As depicted in the diagram, when switch is in ON position, electric current is passed through the coil or solenoid. By the phenomenon of magnetic effect of current, the coil or solenoid gets magnetised which attracts nearby soft iron armature and the hammer strikes the gong to produce a sound.

Thus, electric bell starts ringing and as soon as switch is OFF, no current flows through the coil and its magnetisation stops. So, bell stops ringing.

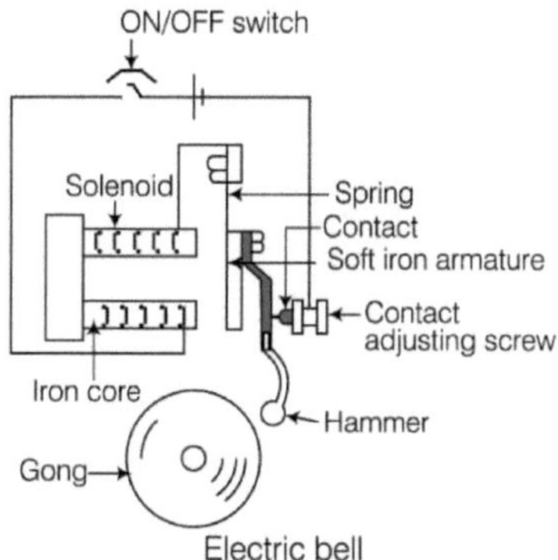

Electric bell

Q. 20 Draw the symbols of the following circuit components.

(a) electric cell (b) switch in OFF position
(c) electric bulb (d) battery

Ans. (a) Electric cell

(b) Switch in OFF position

(c) Electric bulb

(d) Battery

15

Light

Multiple Choice Questions (MCQs)

Q. 1 Boojho and Paheli were given one mirror each by their teacher. Boojho found his image to be erect and of the same size, whereas Paheli found her image erect and smaller in size. This means that the mirrors of Boojho and Paheli are, respectively

(a) plane mirror and concave mirror
(b) concave mirror and convex mirror
(c) plane mirror and convex mirror
(d) convex mirror and plane mirror

Ans. *(c)* As in case of plane mirror, image formed is virtual, erect and of same size and in case of convex mirror, image is virtual, erect and smaller in size.

Q. 2 Which of the following can be used to form a real image?

(a) Only concave mirror
(b) Only plane mirror
(c) Only convex mirror
(d) Both concave and convex mirrors

Ans. *(a)* As only a concave mirror can form a real image. Plane mirror and convex mirror always form a virtual image of an object.

Q. 3 If an object is placed at a distance of 0.5 m in front of a plane mirror, the distance between the object and the image formed by the mirror will be

(a) 2 m (b) 1 m (c) 0.5 m (d) 0.25 m

Ans. *(b)* The image formed by a plane mirror is at the same distance behind the mirror as the object is in front of it. Therefore, the distance between object and image is given by distance between object and mirror + distance between mirror and image

$$= 0.5 \text{ m} + 0.5 \text{ m} = 1 \text{ m}$$

Q. 4 You are provided with a concave mirror, a convex mirror, a concave lens and a convex lens. To obtain an enlarged image of an object, you can use either

(a) concave mirror or convex mirror
(b) concave mirror or convex lens
(c) concave mirror or concave lens
(d) concave lens or convex lens

Ans. *(b)* Concave mirror and convex lens can only form enlarged image of an object. As convex mirror and concave lens always form a diminished image of an object.

Q. 5 A rainbow can be seen in the sky

(a) when the sun is in front of you
(b) when the sun is behind you
(c) when the sun is overhead
(d) only at the time of sunrise

Ans. *(b)* A rainbow can only be seen in the sky when the sun is behind you in rainy season.

Q. 6 An erect and enlarged image can be formed by

(a) only a convex mirror
(b) only a concave mirror
(c) only a plane mirror
(d) both convex and concave mirrors

Ans. *(b)* An erect and enlarged image can only be formed by a concave mirror and it is virtual in nature.

Q. 7 You are provided with a convex mirror, a concave mirror, a convex lens and a concave lens. You can get an inverted image from

(a) both concave lens and convex lens
(b) both concave mirror and convex mirror
(c) both concave mirror and convex lens
(d) both convex mirror and concave lens

Ans. *(c)* Concave mirror and convex lens can only form real and inverted image of an object. As convex mirror and concave lens always form a virtual and erect image of an object.

Q. 8 An image formed by a lens is erect. Such an image could be formed by a

(a) convex lens provided the image is smaller than object
(b) concave lens provided the image is smaller than object
(c) concave lens provided the image is larger than object
(d) concave lens provided the image is of the same size

Ans. *(b)* A concave lens can only form virtual, erect and diminished image of an object. As virtual and erect image formed by a convex lens is always magnified.

Very Short Answer Type Questions

Q. 9 The image formed by a lens is always virtual, erect and smaller in size for an object kept at different positions in front of it. Identify nature of lens.

Ans. Such types of lens which always forms virtual, erect and smaller image in spite of the different positions of an object is called concave lens.

Q. 10 Fill in the blanks.

(a) The inner surface of a steel spoon acts as a .... mirror.
(b) The outer surface of a flat steel plate acts as a .... mirror.
(c) The outer shining surface of a round bottom steel bowl acts as a .... mirror.
(d) The inner surface of the reflector of a torch acts as a .... mirror.

Ans. (a) **Concave** It acts as a concave mirror because it forms real and virtual inverted and erect, magnified and diminished images depending upon the position of an object.

(b) **Plane** It acts as a plane mirror because it forms virtual, erect and same sized image of object.

(c) **Convex** It acts as a convex mirror because it forms virtual, erect and diminished image in spite of the position of an object.

(d) **Concave** It acts as a concave mirror to obtain a parallel beam of light.

Q. 11 State whether the following statement are True or False.

(a) A concave lens can be used to produce an enlarged and erect image.

(b) A convex lens always produces a real image.

(c) The sides of an object and its image formed by a concave mirror are always interchanged.

(d) An object can be seen only if it emits light.

Ans. (a) False, a concave lens can only form virtual, erect and diminished image in spite of the position of object.

(b) False, a convex lens can form real or virtual, inverted or erect magnified and diminished images depending upon the position of object.

(c) True, the image formed by a concave mirror shows lateral inversion, i.e. left seems to be right and right seems to be left.

(d) False, an object can be seen if it reflects the light falling on it.

Short Answer Type Questions

Q. 12 What type of mirror is used as a side mirror in a scooter? Why is this type of mirror chosen?

Ans. Convex mirror is used as a side mirror in a scooter because it can form diminished images of objects spread over a larger area.

So, this helps the driver to have a wide field of view of traffic.

Q. 13 Observe the given figures carefully.

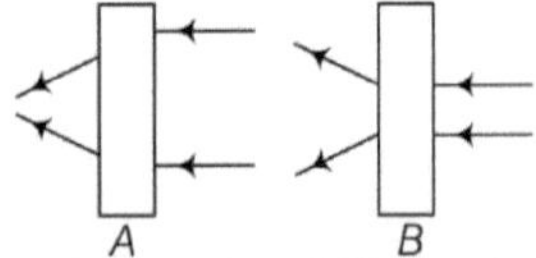

The given figures show the path of light through lenses of two different types represented by rectangular boxes *A* and *B*. What is the nature of lenses *A* and *B*?

Ans. Since, in first case, light rays are converging towards a point, so the lens *A* will be a convex lens and in case of lens *B*, light rays diverge or spread out. So, the lens *B* will be a concave lens.

Q. 14 Boojho made light from a laser torch to fall on a prism. Will he be able to observe a band of seven colours? Explain with a reason.

Ans. No, he will not observe band of seven colours because laser light consists of monochromatic light of a single colour.

However, seven colours of bands are observed, when a white light is passed through a prism and dispersion takes place.

Q. 15 State the correct sequence (1-7) of colours in the spectrum formed by the prisms *A* and *B* shown in the figure.

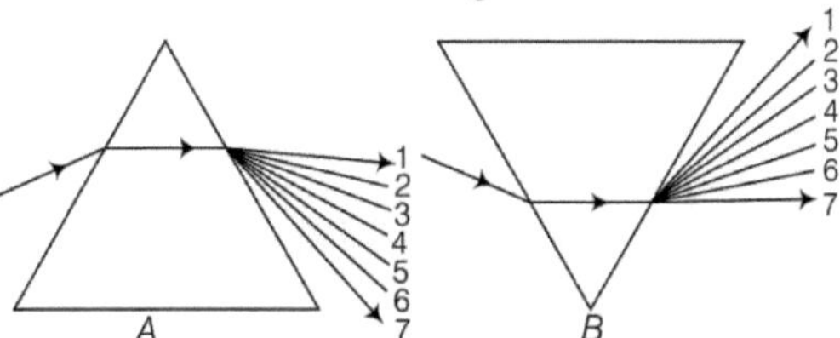

Ans. When a white light is passed through a prism, it disperses into its seven constituent colours.

For *A*	For *B*
1. ⟶ Red	1. ⟶ Violet
2. ⟶ Orange	2. ⟶ Indigo
3. ⟶ Yellow	3. ⟶ Blue
4. ⟶ Green	4. ⟶ Green
5. ⟶ Blue	5. ⟶ Yellow
6. ⟶ Indigo	6. ⟶ Orange
7. ⟶ Violet	7. ⟶ Red

Q. 16 The side mirror of a scooter got broken. The mechanic replaced it with a plane mirror. Mention any inconvenience that the driver of the scooter will face while using it.

Ans. As we know that the side mirror of a scooter must be a convex mirror so that we can view a wide range of traffic spread over a large area.

But if plane mirror, is used, we will not be able to see large area of traffic behind us which may create a difficulty in driving vehicle and can cause accident.

Q. 17 The concave reflecting surface of a torch got rusted. What effect would this have on the beam of light from the torch?

Ans. If the concave reflecting surface of a torch get rusted, it will produce diffused beam of light with lower intensity, the objects will not be clearly visible in this diffused and lower intensity of light.

Q. 18 An erect and enlarged image of an object is formed on a screen. Explain how this could be possible.

Ans. An erect and enlarged image of an object can be formed by either concave mirror or convex lens if an object is placed upside down between the focus and centre of curvature of concave mirror or convex lens.

Q. 19 Two different types of lenses are placed on a sheet of newspaper. How will you identify them without touching?

Ans. On identifying the size of the letters of newspaper, we can differentiate between the two types of lenses.

If image of letters is large or magnified, then the lens is a convex lens and if the image of letters is smaller or diminished in size, then the lens is a concave lens.

Q. 20 A shopkeeper wanted to fix a mirror which will give a maximum view of his shop. What type of mirror should he use? Give reason.

Ans. If a shopkeeper wanted to fix a mirror which will give him maximum view of his shop, he should use a convex mirror.

As a convex mirror can form images of objects spread over a large area, i.e. it can give a wider field of view.

Q. 21 The distance between an object and a convex lens is changing. It is noticed that the size of the image formed on a screen is decreasing. Is the object moving in a direction towards the lens or away from it?

Ans. In case of convex lens, when we move the object away from the lens, the size of image decreases and ultimately, when object is at infinite distance a point image is formed at the focus of lens.

Long Answer Type Questions

Q. 22 Suppose we wish to obtain the real image of a distant tree. Explain two possible ways in which we can do it.

Ans. (i) In first case, we will use a concave mirror and a screen. As we know that a concave mirror forms a real image of a distant object at its focus, therefore, a real image of a distance tree will be formed on the screen placed at the focus of concave mirror.

(ii) In second case, we will use a convex lens and a screen. As convex lens forms a real image of a distant object at its focus, therefore, a real image of a distant tree will be formed on the screen placed at the focus of convex lens.

Q. 23 It was observed that when the distance between an object and a lens decreases, the size of the image increases. What is the nature of this lens? If you keep on decreasing the distance between the object and the lens, will you still able to obtain the image on the screen? Explain.

Ans. If on decreasing the distance between the object and lens, the size of the image increases, then the nature of the lens is convex type.

No, if the distance between object and lens is less than the focal length of the lens, then it will form a virtual image which cannot be obtained on a screen.

Q. 24 You are given three mirrors of different types. How will you identify each one of them?

Ans. We can identify the mirrors by forming images of an object which are given as below:

(i) **Plane mirror** In case of plane mirror, image will be virtual, erect and of same size as that of object.

(ii) **Concave mirror** In case of concave mirror, image may be real or virtual, inverted or erect and magnified or diminished depending upon the position of object.

(iii) **Convex mirror** In case of convex mirror, image formed will always be virtual, erect and diminished in spite of the position of object.

16

Water : A Precious Resource

Multiple Choice Questions (MCQs)

Q. 1 Which of the following does not show water shortage?

(a) Taps running dry
(b) Long queues for getting water
(c) Marches and protests for demand of water
(d) A family gets three buckets of water per person per day

Ans. *(d)* According to the recommendation of United Nations (UN) minimum 50 litres of water per person per day should be provided.

Hence, three buckets (nearly 60 litres) of water is sufficient for a person for one day.

Q. 2 Seas and oceans are full of water on earth. However a very small percentage of water present on earth is available for us. This percentage is roughly.

(a) 0.006% (b) 0.06% (c) 0.6% (d) 6%

Ans. *(a)* Most of the water present on earth is not fit for consumption by us. Sea and oceans contain salty water which cannot be drunk. Even most of the fresh water is frozen as ice in glaciers and polar regions.

Hence, we are left with limited amount of water from lake, river and under the ground.

Q. 3 Which of the following are not the liquid forms of water?

(i) Snow (ii) Lake water
(iii) River water (iv) Water vapour
(v) Ice

Choose the correct combination from the options below

(a) (i), (iv) and (v) (b) (i) and (ii) (c) (ii) and (iii) (d) (iv) only

Ans. *(a)* Snow and ice are frozen while water vapour is in gaseous state. Water from lake and river are in liquid state.

Q. 4 A man digging the ground near a waterbody found that the soil was moist. As he kept digging deeper and deeper he reached a level, where all the spaces between particles of soil and gaps between rocks were filled with water. The upper limit of this layer is called

(a) water level (b) water table
(c) groundwater (d) water limit

Ans. *(b)* The upper limit of the layer where water is present between particles of soil and gaps between rocks is called water table and water below this layer is called groundwater.

Q. 5 Which of the following is a way to use water economically?

(a) Construction of bawris (b) Rainwater harvesting
(c) Drip irrigation (d) Infiltration

Ans. *(c)* Among the given options, drip irrigation is a way to use water economically because the installation of drip irrigation techniques require less amount of water.

Q. 6 On which of the following day is World Water Day observed?

(a) 22 March (b) 14 November
(c) 2 October (d) 21 December

Ans. *(a)* 22 March is celebrated as the World Water Day.

Q. 7 The amount of water recommended by the United Nations for drinking, washing, cooking and maintaining proper hygiene per person per day is a minimum of

(a) 5 L (b) 15 L
(c) 30 L (d) 50 L

Ans. *(d)* The amount of water recommended by the United Nations for drinking, washing, cooking and maintaining proper hygiene is a minimum of 50 litres per person per day.

Q. 8 'Every Drop Counts' is a slogan related to

(a) counting of drops of any liquid (b) counting of water drops
(c) importance of water (d) importance of counting

Ans. *(c)* Every drop of water is precious for life to sustain on earth.

Q. 9 Water cycle does not involve which of the following?

(a) Evaporation (b) Condensation
(c) Formation of clouds (d) Rainwater harvesting

Ans. *(d)* Water cycle does not involve rainwater harvesting. Rainwater harvesting involves recharging the groundwater.

Q. 10 Which of the following inhibits the seepage of rainwater into ground?

(a) A pukka floor (b) Playground
(c) Grass lawn (d) Forest land

Ans. *(a)* A pukka or cemented floor is usually impervious to water, inhibiting the seepage of rainwater into grounds.

Very Short Answer Type Questions

Q. 11 State whether True/False.

(a) Water vapour is the gaseous form of water.

(b) Ice is solid, whereas snow is the semi-solid form of water.

(c) Ocean water cannot be used for domestic purposes.

(d) Rapid growth of industries is one of the cause for water shortage.

Ans. (a) True (b) False, snow is also solid form of water.
(c) True (d) True

Q. 12 Some definitions are given which can be corrected by changing one word. Correct them.

(a) Aquifer is groundwater stored between layers of hard rock above the water table.

(b) The process of evaporation of water in the ground is called infiltration.

(c) The evaporation of water from oceans and its arrival back into oceans is called vapour cycle.

Ans. (a) Aquifer is groundwater stored between layers of hard rock **below** the water table.

(b) The process of **seeping** of water in the ground is called infiltration.

(c) The evaporation of water from oceans and its arrival back into oceans is called **water cycle**.

Q. 13 What is the source of water in each of the following?

(a) Wells (b) Ground (c) Atmosphere

Ans. (a) The source of water in wells is groundwater.

(b) The source of water on ground is rain.

(c) The source of water in atmosphere is evaporation.

Q. 14 State whether True/False.

(a) The process of seeping of water into ground is called filtration.

(b) 51% of the earth's surface is covered with water.

(c) Year 2003 was observed as the International year of freshwater.

(d) Snow and ice both are solid form of water.

Ans. (a) False, the process of seeping of water into the ground is called infiltration.

(b) False, 71% of earth surface is covered with water.

(c) True

(d) True

Short Answer Type Questions

Q. 15 The rainwater and ... from other sources such as rivers and ponds seep through the ... and fills the empty spaces and cracks deep below the ground. The process of seeping of water into the ground is called ... .

Ans. *(c)* water, soil, infiltration

Q. 16 Rajasthan is a ... and dry place. The challenge of natural ... of water was met by a successful experiment. A band of social ... had transformed a ... area into a green place. They have revived five dried-up ... by constructing water ... structures.

Ans. hot, scarcity, workers, dry, rivers, harvesting.

Q. 17 Place the following statements in a proper order to form a meaningful paragraph.

(a) Which inturn decreases the seepage of rainwater into the ground.

(b) This decreases the open areas like parks and playgrounds.

(c) Increasing population create demand for construction of houses, shops, offices, roads and pavements.

(d) This results in depletion of water table and creates scarcity of more water.

Ans. Increasing population create demand for construction of houses, shops, offices, roads and pavements (c). This decreases the open areas like parks and playgrounds (b), which inturn decreases the seepage of rainwater into the ground (a).

This result in depletion of water table and creates scarcity of more water (d).

Q. 18 How can you observe the three forms of water (a) in nature and (b) at home?

Ans. The three forms of water

(a) in nature are snow (solid), water (liquid) and water vapour (gas).

(b) at home are ice (solid), water (liquid) and steam (gas).

Q. 19 Complete the given table.

	Form of water	Process by which formed	Location where found
(a)	Liquid		
(b)	Solid		
(c)	Gaseous		

Ans. The complete table is given below:

	Form of water	Process by which formed	Location where found
(a)	Liquid	Condensation and melting	Waterbodies like rivers, lakes, etc.
(b)	Solid	Freezing	Cold regions like high mountains, polar regions, etc.
(c)	Gaseous	Evaporation	Atmosphere

Q. 20 Match the Column I with Column II.

Column I		Column II	
(a)	Groundwater	(i)	Solid form of water
(b)	Bawri	(ii)	Wastage of water
(c)	Snow	(iii)	Water management
(d)	Drip irrigation	(iv)	Small waterbody
(e)	Leaking taps	(v)	Water table

Ans. The correct matching is as given

(a)—(v), (b)—(iv), (c)—(i), (d)—(iii), (e)—(ii)

Q. 21 A list of jumbled words are given here, write the correct form of each word.

(a) WASHFERRET (b) CHARREGE (c) QUIFERA (d) WOSN

Ans. (a) FRESH WATER (b) RECHARGE

(c) AQUIFER (d) SNOW

Q. 22 From where do the following usually get water? In which form is water present in them?

(a) Clouds (b) Plants

(c) Mountain tops (d) Aquifer

(e) Animals

Ans.

	Source of water	Form of water
Clouds	Land	Liquid form (droplet of water)
Plants	Soil	Liquid form
Mountain tops	Atmosphere	Solid form
Aquifer	Rain	Underground water
Animals	Waterbodies	Liquid

Long Answer Type Questions

Q. 23 Complete the following chart by writing appropriate words in the boxes marked (a) to (e).

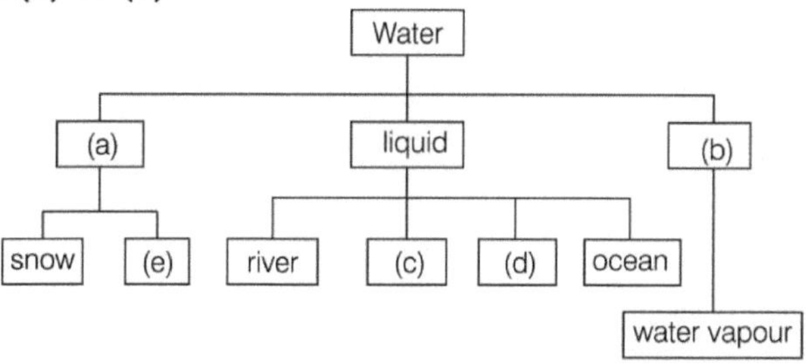

Ans. (a) Solid (b) Gaseous
(c) Well (d) Lake
(e) Ice

Q. 24 What is groundwater? What are the sources of water which are fed by groundwater?

Ans. Water below the water table where water is found between particles of soil and between rocks is called groundwater. Water table is the upper level of water under the ground which occupies all the spaces in the soil and rocks.

The ground water provide water to wells, bawris, tube wells, hand pumps.

Q. 25 Water is very precious for all the living beings. What will happen in future, if we do not save water now?

Ans. Water is needed for various life activities. If we continue the misuse of water and do not conserve it, the groundwater level will be depleted. This may result into various consequences like:

(i) **Lowering of the water table** Excessive pumping can lower the groundwater table.

(ii) **Reduced surface water supply** Groundwater and surface water are connected. When groundwater is over used, the lakes, streams and rivers connected to groundwater, can also have little supply.

(iii) **Loss of plants from land** We fully depend on the plants for food directly or indirectly. Plants need water to prepare their food. If there will be scarcity of water on earth, the plants will be unable to prepare their food. This inturn will lead to the end of the life because world without plants means no food, no oxygen, not enough rain and other innumerable problems.

Therefore, it is true that water is a precious resource.

17

Forests : Our Lifeline

Multiple Choice Questions (MCQs)

Q. 1 Which of the following serve as green lungs?

(a) Green pigment of the plants (b) Forests
(c) Kitchen gardens (d) Greenhouse gases

Ans. *(b)* Forests serve as green lungs as they produce oxygen for breathing and respiration and help in maintaining oxygen and carbon dioxide balance in the atmosphere.

Q. 2 Boojho visited a forest near his town with his classmates and his teacher. As they were entering the forest, their class teacher told them not to make noise in the forest as noise could disturb the

(a) birds (b) animals
(c) Both (a) and (b) (d) plants

Ans. *(c)* As Boojho was entering the forest, his class teacher told him not to make noise in the forest because it could disturb both birds and animals.

Q. 3 Which among the following forests animals is the smallest?

(a) Fox (b) Boar
(c) Bison (d) Porcupine

Ans. *(d)* Porcupine is the smallest forest animal among the following given in the options.

Q. 4 Which of the following has the strongest stem?

(a) A tree (b) A creeper (c) A climber (d) A bush

Ans. *(a)* A tree has the strongest stem.

Q. 5 Which of the following is not prepared from the wood obtained from forest?

(a) Paper (b) Thermocol (c) Matchsticks (d) Plywood

Ans. *(b)* Thermocol is not prepared from the wood obtained from the forest. Paper, matchsticks and plywood are prepared from the wood.

Q. 6 Which of the following is not the name of a tree?

(a) Teak (b) Sal (c) Porcupine (d) Kachnar

Ans. *(c)* Porcupine is not the name of a tree rather it is an animal. Teak, sal and kachnar are names of trees.

Q. 7 Pick the option which gives the names of a tree and an animal respectively from the following.

(a) Semal and hornbill (b) Sal and khair
(c) Chinkara and blue bull (d) Neem and palash

Ans. *(a)* From the above given options, semal and hornbill are the names of a tree and an animal, respectively.

Q. 8 Which of the products is not obtained from a forest?

(a) Honey (b) Catechu (c) Gum (d) Ginger

Ans. *(d)* Honey, catechu (kattha) and gum are forest products but ginger is not a forest product.

Q. 9 The branchy part of a tree above the stem is know as

(a) Crown (b) Canopy (c) Sapling (d) Humus

Ans. *(a)* The branchy part of a tree above the stem is known as the crown of the tree. The crown includes the top part of a tree which has all the branches and leaves of the tree.

Q. 10 Forests are not responsible for

(a) providing medicinal plants
(b) maintaining the flow of water into the streams
(c) creating flood conditions
(d) absorbing rainwater and maintaining water table

Ans. *(c)* Forests are not responsible for creating flood conditions, as they protect form flood condition.

Very Short Answer Type Questions

Q. 11 Paheli while moving in a forest observed that there was no noise pollution, though lots of heavy vehicles were passing from the nearby highway. Explain why.

Ans. Paheli observed that there was no noise pollution in a forest even though there were lots of heavy vehicles passing from the nearby highway. It is because trees present in the forest absorb the noise.

Q. 12 State whether the following statements are true or false. If false give the correct statement.

(a) Forest influence climate, water cycle and air quality.
(b) In a forest, trees form the uppermost layer, followed by herbs. The shrubs form the lowest layer of vegetation.
(c) The forest keeps on growing and changing and can regenerate.
(d) Forest protect the soil from erosion.

Ans. (a) True

(b) False, in a forest, trees form the uppermost layer followed by shrubs. The herbs form the lowest layer of vegetation.

(c) True

(d) True

Q. 13 Paheli wrote a food chain in the following way:

Frog → Eagle → Insects → Grass → Snake

The chain is not in the correct order. Help her to write the food chain correctly.

Ans. The correct food chain is:

Grass → Insects → Frog → Snake → Eagle

An insect eats green plant or grass – a frog eats the insects – the frog is eaten by snake – the snake is eaten by an eagle.

Short Answer Type Questions

Q. 14 Give names of any four birds which you expect to see in a forest.

Ans. The four birds which we expect to see in a forest are jungle crow, hornbill, myna and koel.

Q. 15 Two friends shared their experiences of their vacation trip to two different forests. Do you think they would have seen the same type of plants and animals during their respective trips? Give reason.

Ans. No, they would not have seen the same type of plants and animals. This is so, because climatic conditions in the two forests would vary leading to variations in the types of plants and animals.

Q. 16 A bunch of seedlings were seen sprouting on a heap of animal dropping in a forest. How do you think is the seedling benefited from the animal dung?

Ans. The seedling was being benefited from the animal dung as the decaying animal dung provided nutrients to the growing seedlings. This happens as follows–Animal dung or droppings keep on collecting on the forest floor. The decomposer organism (such as bacteria of fungi) act on animal wastes and convert them into humus.

The humus contains plant nutrients and it mixes with the forest soil and make it fertile, seeds obtain nutrients from forest soil and germinate to form seedlings and seedlings grow to form saplings.

Q. 17 Match the Column I with Column II.

	Column I		Column II
(a)	Decomposers	(i)	Dead plant and animal tissues
(b)	Canopy	(ii)	Habitats for wildlife
(c)	Porcupine	(iii)	Microorganisms
(d)	Humus	(iv)	Wild animal
(e)	Forest	(v)	Branches of tall trees

Ans. The correct matching is as given:

(a)—(ii), (b)—(v), (c)—(iv), (d)—(i), (e)—(ii)

Q. 18 Deforestation may lead to floods. Why?

Ans. Deforestation leads to floods as lesser number of trees will be available due to the deforestation. In the absence of trees and plants of the forest, the excessive amount of rainwater falling during heavy rains cannot be absorbed into forest ground. The large amount of rainwater will then suddenly flow into rivers causing the flooding of rivers.

Q. 19 Name any four useful products other than wood, which we get from forests.

Ans. Four useful products other than wood which we get from forests are gum, spices, fodder for animals and medicinal plants.

Long Answer Type Questions

Q. 20 Figure shows a part of a forest.

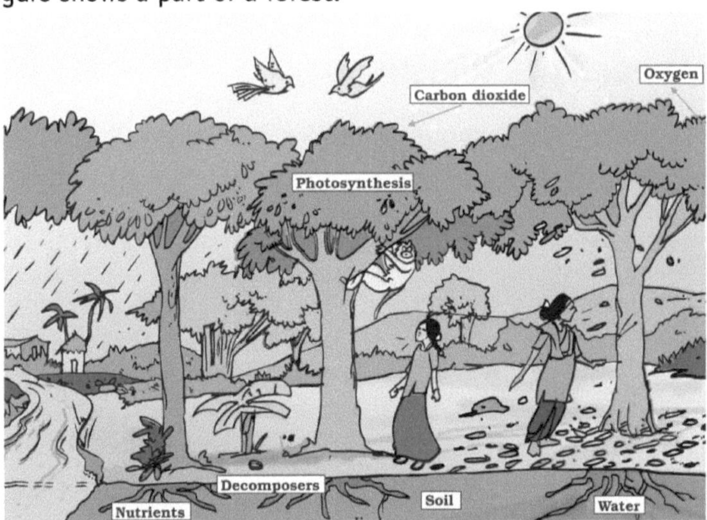

Write any three activities going on in the forest on the basis of this figure.

Ans. The three activities going on in the forest on the basis of the given figure are:

(i) Oxygen is given out by plant leaves.

(ii) Carbon dioxide is consumed by the plants to prepare their food by the process of photosynthesis.

(iii) Nutrients are being added to the soil by the action of decomposers.

Q. 21 People say that nothing goes waste in a forest. Can you explain how?

Ans. Nothing goes waste in a forest because of the following reasons:

(i) Dry leaves and remains of dead animals are converted to a dark coloured substance called humus and increase the fertility of soil. The importance of humus to the soil is that it provide nutrients for the growth of plants.

(ii) Dead animals become food for vultures, crows, jackals and insects.

(iii) Broken branches of trees are used as fuel by the people living in the vicinity of the forest.

Q. 22 Give any four factors which are responsible for the destruction of forests.

Ans. The four factors which are responsible for the destruction of forests are:

(i) Construction of roads.
(ii) Construction of buildings.
(iii) Industrial development.
(iv) Increasing demand of wood.

Q. 23 Draw a figure showing two animals, two birds and a few trees as a part of a forest.

Ans. Here is a figure showing two animals, two birds and a few trees as a part of forest:

Q. 24 All the needs of animals living in a forest are fulfilled. Justify this statement in a few sentences.

Ans. Forest provides home (shelter), food and water to the animals living there. There are a large number of various types of animals in the forest. The forests provide a natural habitat to animals. The different layers of regulation present in a forest provide food and shelter. Forest provides leaves, flowers, fruits, seeds, nuts and bark of trees as food for herbivorous animals. The carnivorous animals hunt and eat herbivorous animals. The dense bushes, tall grasses and thick trees provides shelter and also protection for herbivorous animals.

Q. 25 Forests are valuable resources. Explain.

Ans. Forest products play vital role in socio-economic development. We get food (cereals, pulses and fruits), fire wood, fibre, construction material, industrial products (tannins, lubricants, dyes, resins and perfumes) and products of medicinal importance. It is also the home of diverse wildlife which maintains the ecosystem.

Forests give oxygen to keep us alive and absorb carbon dioxide and it also help in maintaining water cycle in nature. Forests save the soil from erosion and help in maintaining the ground water level.

Thus, forests are valuable resources.

18

Wastewater Story

Multiple Choice Questions (MCQs)

Q. 1 Which of the following is wastewater?

(a) Water trickling from a damaged tap
(b) Water coming out of a shower
(c) Water flowing in a river
(d) Water coming out of a laundry

Ans. *(d)* Water coming out of a laundry is wastewater.

Q. 2 Sewage is mainly a

(a) liquid waste (b) solid waste
(c) gaseous waste (d) mixture of solid and gas

Ans. *(a)* Sewage is mainly a liquid waste. The waste water and faeces from homes and other buildings which is carried away in sewers, is called sewage.

Q. 3 Which of the following is/are products of wastewater treatment?

(a) Biogas (b) Sludge
(c) Both biogas and sludge (d) Aerator

Ans. *(c)* Biogas and sludge both are the products of wastewater treatment.

Q. 4 Open drain system is a breeding place for which of the following?

(a) Flies (b) Mosquitoes
(c) Organisms which cause diseases (d) All of these

Ans. *(d)* Open drain system is a breeding place for flies, mosquitoes and organisms which cause diseases.

Q. 5 Water polluted by various human activities causes a number of water-borne diseases. Which of the following is not a water borne disease?

(a) Cholera (b) Typhoid (c) Asthma (d) Dysentry

Ans. *(c)* Asthma is not a water-borne disease. It is caused by polluted air.

Q. 6 Pick from the following one chemical which is used to disinfect water.

(a) Chlorine (b) Washing soda (c) Silica (d) Coal

Ans. ***(a)*** Chlorine is the chemical used as water disinfectant.

Q. 7 The system of a network of pipes used for taking away wastewater from homes or public buildings to the treatment plant is known as

(a) sewers (b) sewerage (c) transport system (d) treatment plant

Ans. ***(b)*** The system of a network of pipes used for taking away wastewater from homes or public buildings to the treatment plant is known as sewerage.

Q. 8 Which of the following is a part of inorganic impurities of the sewage?

(a) Pesticides (b) Urea (c) Phosphates (d) Vegetable waste

Ans. ***(c)*** Phosphate is an inorganic impurity of the sewage.

Q. 9 In a filtration plant, water is filtered using layers of

(a) sand and clay (b) clay and fine gravel
(c) sand and fine gravel (d) sand, fine gravel and medium gravel

Ans. ***(d)*** In a filtration plant, water is filtered using layers of sand, fine gravel and medium gravel.

Q. 10 Which of the following is not a source of wastewater?

(a) Sewers (b) Homes (c) Industries (d) Hospitals

Ans. ***(a)*** Sewers are not considered as sources of wastewater. Homes, industries and hospitals are considered as a source of wastewater.

Very Short Answer Type Questions

Q. 11 Why open drains is a concern?

Ans. Open drain is a big concern for the society because they create unhygienic conditions and flies, mosquitoes and other insects breed can spread a number of diseases.

Q. 12 State whether the following statements are True or False. In case a statements is false, write the correct statement.

1. Sewage is a solid waste which causes water pollution and soil pollution.
2. Used water is wastewater.
3. Wastewater could be reused.
4. Where underground sewerage systems and refuse disposal systems are not available, the high cost onsite sanitation system can be adopted.

Ans. (a) False, sewage is a liquid waste which causes water pollution and soil pollution.

(b) True

(c) True

(d) False, where underground sewerage systems and refuse disposal systems are not available, the low cost onsite sanitation system can be adopted.

Q. 13 How are open drains harmful for human health?

Ans. Open drain system creates the most unhygienic and unsanitary conditions in its neighbourhood. Open dirty water drains are breeding places for flies, mosquitoes and other disease causing organism.

Short Answer Type Questions

Q. 14 Name two inorganic impurities present in sewage.

Ans. Inorganic impurities present in sewage are nitrates and phosphates.

Q. 15 Animal waste, oil and urea are some of the organic impurities present in sewage. Name two more organic impurities present in sewage.

Ans. Fruits and vegetable wastes, pesticides and herbicides are organic impurities present in sewage other than animal wastes, oil and urea.

Q. 16 Name two alternative arrangements for sewage disposal where there is no sewerage system.

Ans. The two alternative arrangements for sewage disposal, where there is no sewerage are as below:

(i) Septic tanks (ii) Composting pits

Q. 17 A man travelling in a train threw an empty packet of food on the platform. Do you think this is a proper waste disposal method? Elaborate.

Ans. No, one must always put the waste in a nearby dustbin or carry it home and dispose it in dustbins there.

Waste, not properly disposed may enter into the drains and choke them. It also makes public places dirty and unhygienic.

Q. 18 Why should we not throw

(a) used tea leaves into sink? (b) cooking oil and fats down the drain?

Ans. (a) We should not throw used tea leaves into sink because it may choke the drain-pipe of the sink and do not allow the free fall of waste water through them.

(b) We should not throw cooking oil and fats down the drain because cooking oil and fats down the drain as it can harden and block the drainage pipes. And in an open drain, the fats clog the soil pores reducing its effectiveness in filtering water.

Q. 19 Match the Column I with Column II.

Column I	Column II
(a) Inorganic impurities	(i) Phosphorus and nitrogen
(b) Organic impurities	(ii) Nitrates and phosphates
(c) Nutrients	(iii) Cholera and typhoid
(d) Bacteria	(iv) Pesticides and herbicides

Ans. The correct matching is as given:
(a)—(ii), (b)—(iv), (c)—(i), (d)—(iii)

Q. 20 Given below is a jumbled sequence of the processes involved in a wastewater treatment plant. Arrange them in their correct sequence.

(a) Sludge is scraped out and skimmer removes floating grease.
(b) Water is made to settle in a large tank with a slope in the middle.
(c) Large objects like plastic bags are removed by passing wastewater through bar screens.
(d) Sand, grit and pebbles are made to settle by decreasing the speed of incoming wastewater.
(e) Wastewater enters a grit and sand removal tank.

Ans. The correct sequence of wastewater treatment in treatment plant is:

(c) Large objects like plastic bags are removed by passing wastewater through bar screens.
(e) Wastewater enters a grit and sand removal tank.
(d) Sand, grit and pebbles are made to settle by decreasing the speed of incoming wastewater.
(b) Water is made to settle in a large tank with a slope in the middle.
(a) Sludge is scraped out and skimmer removes the floating grease.

Q. 21 Three statements are provided here which define the terms, i.e. sludge, sewage and wastewater.

Pick out the correct definition for each of these terms.

(a) The settled solids that are removed in wastewater treatment with a scraper.
(b) Water from kitchen used for washing dishes.
(c) Wastewater released from homes, industries, hospitals and other public buildings.

Ans. (a) The settled solids that are removed in wastewater treatment with a scraper is sludge.
(b) Water from kitchen which is used for washing dishes is wastewater.
(c) Wastewater released from homes, industries, hospitals and other public buildings is sewage.

Q. 22 A mixture (x) in water contains suspended solids, organic impurities, inorganic impurities (a), nutrients (b), disease causing bacteria and other microbes. Give names for (x), (a) and (b)?

Ans. A mixture of **sewage** (x) in water contains suspended solids, organic impurities, inorganic impurities like **nitrates, phosphates and metals** (a), nutrients like **phosphorus and nitrogen** (b), disease causing bacteria and other microbes.

Long Answer Type Questions

Q. 23 What are the different types of inorganic and organic impurities generally present in sewage?

Ans. The different types of inorganic and organic impurities present in sewage are as below:

(i) Inorganic impurities - nitrates, phosphates and metals.

(ii) Organic impurities - fruit and vegetable wastes, oil, urea, human faeces, animal waste, pesticides and herbicides.

Q. 24 The terms 'sewage', 'sewers' and 'sewerage' are interlinked with each other. Can you explain, how?

Ans. The terms like 'sewage', 'sewers' and 'sewerage' are interlinked with each other because sewage is a mixture of wastewater coming out of homes and other places.

Sewers are pipes which carry sewage and sewerage is a network of sewage carrying pipes.

Q. 25 A very ... number of our people defecate in the open. It may cause ... pollution and soil pollution. Both the surface water and ... water get polluted. ... water is the source for wells, tubewells and ... . Thus, it becomes most common route for ... borne diseases like ..., dysentery, etc.

Ans. A very **large** number of our people defecate in the open. It may cause **water** pollution and soil pollution. Both the surface water and **groundwater** get polluted.

Groundwater is the source for wells, tubewells and **handpumps**. Thus, it becomes the most common route for **water**-borne diseases like **cholera**, dysentery, etc.

Q. 26 Describe various steps of cleaning wastewater in a wastewater treatment plant.

Ans. The various steps are:

(a) Wastewater is passed through bar screens. Large objects like rags, sticks, cans, plastic packets, napkins are removed.

(b) Water then goes to a grit and sand removal tank. The speed of the incoming wastewater is decreased to allow sand, grit and pebbles to settle down.

(c) The water is then allowed to settle in a large tank which is sloped towards the middle. Solids like faeces settle at the bottom and are removed with a scraper. This is the **sludge**. A skimmer removes the floatable solids like oil and grease. Water so cleared is called clarified water.

(d) Air is pumped into the clarified water to help aerobic bacteria to grow. Bacteria consume human waste, food waste, soaps and other unwanted matter still remaining in clarified water.

Q. 27 Think and suggest some ways to minimise waste and pollutants at their source, taking your home as an example.

Ans. We can minimise waste and pollutants entering the water and create less wastewater by taking following few steps at home:

(i) By not throwing used tea leaves, solid food remains, etc. in the drain. We should throw it in the dustbin.

(ii) By not throwing chemicals like medicines, paints, insecticides, etc. in the drain as they increase the pollution load of the sewage.

9 789352 511501

Printed by Libri Plureos GmbH in Hamburg,
Germany